Character Under Construction

By Donna B. Forrest, Ed.S., L.P.C.

Cover Design by Elizabeth Madden
Layout by Melinda Boyle and Elizabeth Madden
Project Editing by Susan Bowman

ISBN - 1-889636-19-3

Library of Congress Number
99-67577

10 9 8 7 6 5 4 3 2 1
Printed in the United States

YouthLight, Inc.
P.O. Box 115 • Chapin, South Carolina 29036
(800) 209-9774 • (803) 345-1070
Fax (803) 345-0888 • Email YLDR1@aol.com
www.youthlight.com

Children develop
Character by what
they see, by what
they hear, and by
what they are
repeatedly led
to do.

-- James Stenson

ACKNOWLEDGEMENTS

In order for this book to become a reality and for my passion as an advocate for Character Education to continue, there are certain people that have been instrumental and must be recognized.

Bob and Susan Bowman are a "team" of encouragers -- always at the end of the telephone, always full of ideas, and very polite when my ideas needed refining!

My children, April and Derek, are simply remarkable. April re-typed this entire manuscript and kept the house very neat as I worked. Derek manages to work, go to school, and keep my yards neat – to both my appreciation and my neighbor's relief! Daily these two practice forgiveness for my many character flaws.

Then there is Margaret, Lenzy, Eleanor, and Allen who keep constant "watch" over my own character! Such Christian role models with high character standards are priceless and words cannot adequately express what their support means to me!

My parents, George and Claudine, have taught by modeling perseverance, goal setting, responsibility, and courage. Neither of these two ever give up!

This would not be complete without the recognition of Jenny, Paige, Patricia, Jay, Libby, Rita, Sandi, and "Mema". Also, the staff of Merriwether Elementary School and Community Care and Counseling of North August exhibit wonderful character traits for the children within their care. When I think of Character – especially friendship and kindness – these many individuals exhibit so many traits I wish to emulate!

Thanks to all of you!
Donna

Table of Contents

Introduction

The curriculum of any school – public or private – can be greatly enhanced by the inclusion of a Character Education program to begin in Kindergarten. As a society, unfortunately, we can no longer assume that children understand the concepts of responsibility, respect of self and others, courage, kindness, and other positive character traits.

The intent of the virtues taught in Character Education is to supplement the home environment – not change values – and encourage virtues needed to live an entire life span to the fullest possible degree. These virtues stress the importance of positive life styles and the choices we have before us – no matter who we are or where we have lived.

Intended as an all-in-one resource for elementary school teachers, counselors, and other caring professionals wanting to implement Character Education into the every day curriculum, *Character Under Construction* offers a wonderfully unique approach. One-of-a-kind detailed lesson plans (some of which include bulletin board ideas), parent letters, children's literature ideas, and daily statements taken from *180 Days of Character* are included in each of the sections.

While use in any Kindergarten through 6th grade classroom setting is the original intent of the author, it has been found to work well in small group settings. The lessons can be easily interwoven into the daily curriculum either by following directly the book formats or by individualizing to fit the specific needs of the class/school populations.

Repetition is a proven technique in teaching elementary aged children. However, the variations offered in this book will improve student motivation. Lesson plan formats are complete and easy to follow. A brief overview, materials and time needed are listed, objectives covered, complete procedures written out, follow-up questions offered, optional endings given, some bulletin board ideas, and home/parent letters are included in each section.

Taken from the original *180 Days of Character*, the 180 character keys under the headings are included for convenient implementation on a daily basis. Also, following this introduction on pages xi thru xiv, are the character keys which can be reproduced, cut out and posted in the classroom for referral during the lessons.

Variations included in these lessons plans contain different play therapy techniques (such as role play, rapping, poetry, drawing, puppets, etc.). Each learning style is covered in order to gain the attention of all students.

Since schools are second, only to the home, in the development of children's character, then we must teach the choices available to every human. In summary, **we are our choices and our choices make up our character!**

CHARACTER KEYS

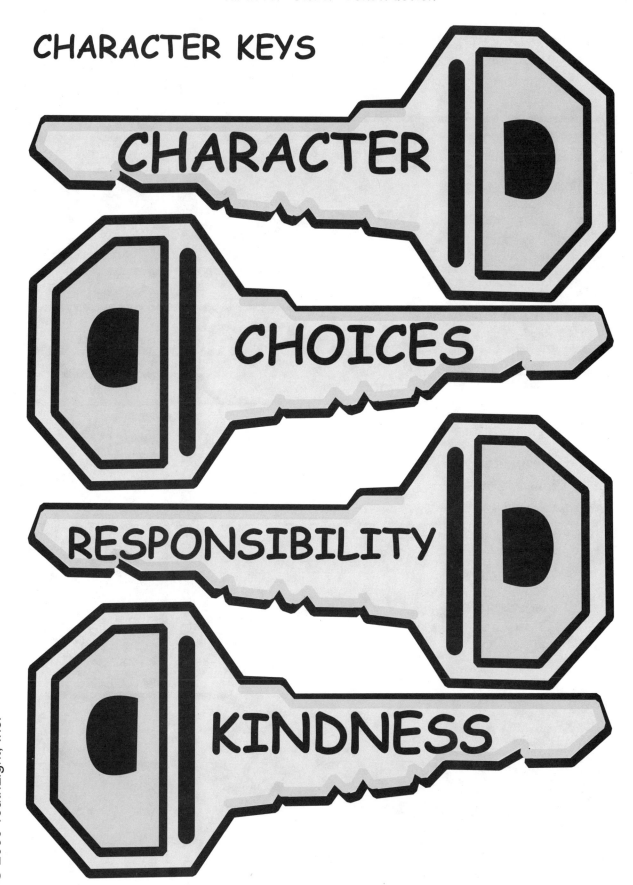

CHARACTER KEYS

CHARACTER KEYS

CHARACTER KEYS

DEPENDABILITY

POSITIVE ATTITUDE

xiv

CHARACTER BLUEPRINT

🔑 Keys to CHARACTER

🔑 Your character is who you really are inside yourself.

🔑 Good character traits can become good life habits!

🔑 Good life habits can lead toward a better life!

🔑 Your good character can never be taken away from you by anyone but *you*!

🔑 Character involves the way you deal with yourself and others - both on the outside and the inside.

🔑 Good character equals more life success.

🔑 Good character helps maintain integrity through both good and bad times.

🔑 Good character is supported by a positive attitude.

🔑 Appear positive, think positive, act positive and the character of those around you will improve!

🔑 Gain peace inside yourself by practicing good character traits such as honesty, respect, responsibility and courage.

Character Blueprint

(Sample Parent Letter)

Dear Parent(s)/Guardian(s):

During this year our class will be discussing "Good Character Traits". We will be recognizing children who are kind, truthful, show respect toward others, are responsible, use good manners, and much more!

Our theme is "CHARACTER UNDER CONSTRUCTION" and this first section is the beginning blueprint! Just as you and I have grown and matured over the last several decades, our children need to be shown that as they grow they will make mistakes. But if they keep "BUILDING" on good character it will help them become more successful in life and have many more friends!

Your help will be so valuable to these life lessons! Please encourage your child to practice these good character traits at home. PRAISE good character changes that your child makes as he/she matures!

More information will be sent to you as we study and learn about each individual character trait. Please send me a note with any success you notice at home from this character program so I can reinforce and praise your child's progress, too! Thanks for your participation and support!

My best,

Activity 1:
CHARACTER CART

BRIEF OVERVIEW

This lesson is a simple overview and awareness exercise of positive character traits such as making good choices, being responsible and kind, showing respect, having courage, etc. It is to be the foundational introduction to the more detailed character lessons contained in this book.

MATERIALS NEEDED

- "CART" worksheet
- Card stock paper (various colors)
- Safety scissors
- Quick dry glue (or scotch tape)

TIME NEEDED

30 minutes

OBJECTIVE

Students are introduced and will recognize good character virtues.

PROCEDURES

Copy on different colored paper the "CART" worksheet so that each student will have a copy. An example of a completed "CART" will be exhibited for the children to see. The teacher will say the following to the children as she holds up the "CART" (point to each character virtue as it is discussed).

Today we are going to learn about some good character traits that will help us feel better about ourselves. Good character includes things like being honest (or telling the truth). When we tell the truth we can feel good inside ourselves and others listen to us more! Good character includes having good manners and showing respect for other people. We show others good character when we are kind and share with everyone, and we realize everyone is equally important. It is up to each of us to decide or make good choices to show others our good character. When we make these good choices others trust us more and believe we are responsible for the way we choose to act! A good attitude is very important and having courage to do the right thing when others want us to break a rule is a must! Let's be dependable and set our goals high for GOOD CHARACTER!

The leader should allow some discussion on the "character vocabulary" and will explain that the class will be learning more about each good character trait throughout the year!

Finally, the leader should instruct the children to cut out the "CART" and four wheels. Once the parts have been cut out, the teacher will show the children how to put the "CART" together.

FOLLOW-UP QUESTIONS:

1. Why do you think the words GOOD CHARACTER is the biggest part of the CART?

2. Can you think of someone special that you know who has good character traits? Tell us which good character trait that person shows you (or several traits).

3. When you work on your own character traits, do you think we can have a better classroom? Why?

OPTIONAL ENDINGS:

K-2 Send home the "CART" with the parent letter for the "Character" chapter as an introduction to our study of good character virtues.

3-5 Ask the principal if the "CARTS" could be displayed in a central place (such as the lunchroom) with a picture of the class in the center and the words "Rolling Toward Good Character"!

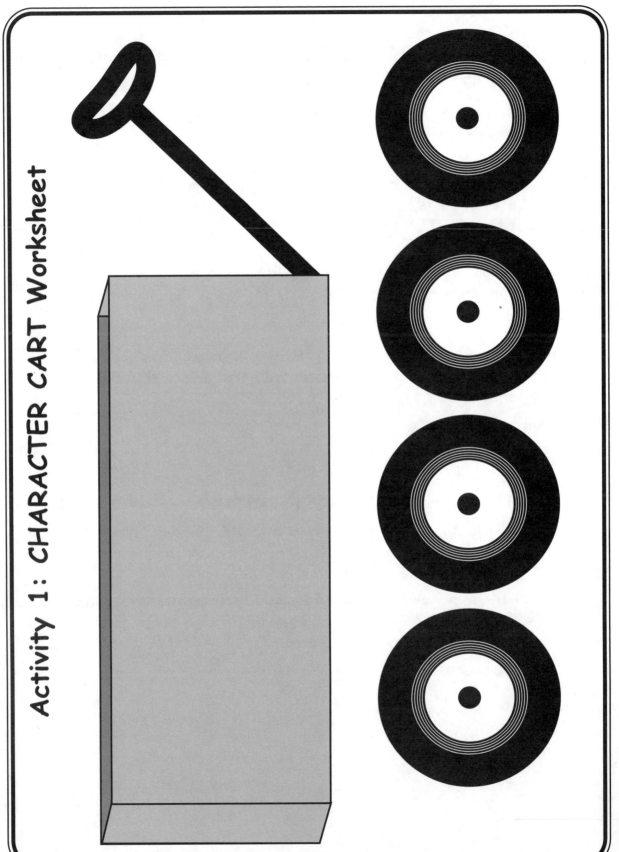

Activity 1: CHARACTER CART Worksheet

Activity 2:
COOL CHARACTER!

BRIEF OVERVIEW

The "Cool Character!" worksheet can be learned by the entire class as a poem or rap. All good character vocabulary words are included in order to familiarize students with the character virtues being explored in this book.

MATERIALS NEEDED

• "Cool Character!" worksheet

TIME NEEDED

30 minutes

OBJECTIVE

Each student will be able to recognize good character vocabulary words. The class will be able to recite the poem (rap) which lists good character trait words.

PROCEDURES

Introduce the class to important good character vocabulary words (can be found in bold print in the "Cool Character" poem). The leader should hold a class discussion about these words. For example, with the word "CHOICES" - "Good choices are available to everyone" or "We need to make good choices BEFORE we ACT". It should be stressed that if each class member practices good character actions, our class will be a nicer place!

Students should then be challenged to learn the "Cool Character" poem (rap). This could be practiced at various times throughout the day for several consecutive days. When the class recites the poem with enthusiasm, encourage them to go to another classroom and share the poem (rap) with other students!

FOLLOW-UP QUESTIONS

1. Which good character word sounds the most fun to learn about? Why?

2. Tell one good choice you have made either today or yesterday.

3. How can practicing good character traits help you make friends faster?

OPTIONAL ENDINGS

K-2 1. Have the leader write the "Cool Character" poem (rap) on large chart paper. Then have each student draw a picture of a Cool Character to hang around the chart paper.

    2. Make "I'm a Cool Character" badge for children to wear around their neck as they go home for the day. On the back the words could be listed that were discussed during the lesson. These could be copied and cut in any shape (i.e. boy, girl, circle, etc.).

3-5 1. Have students act out the "Cool Character" rap with innovative hand claps, foot taps, etc. This would be especially fun if the class plans to share with other students!

    2. Use the rap on the school morning show or share in the school news paper.

    3. Begin a "Cool Character" club with membership incentives. For example, members get a special Friday treat at lunch or an extra recess during the week. This could be done for an entire grade level with class competitions to see which class has the most members!

COOL CHARACTER!

Making good **CHOICES** really is cool,

It's an important part of being in school!

If you choose to be **RESPONSIBLE** and **KIND**,

More and more friends you will find!

Now in order to gain **RESPECT** and **TRUST**,

You will find being **HONEST** is a must!

We are all **EQUAL** and should learn to **SHARE**

It comes with a good **ATTITUDE** and being fair!

Let's set a **GOAL** and with **COURAGE** pursue,

Being **DEPENDABLE** will be part of me and you!

Including good **MANNERS** is really cool!

Let's have good character at home and school!

Activity 3:
CHARACTER BEING CONSTRUCTED HERE!

BRIEF OVERVIEW

As children grow they need to be aware that everyone makes mistakes. Through these mistakes we can learn and our character builds! It takes little steps forward (and a few backward) to reach our goal of becoming people of good character.

MATERIALS NEEDED

- "Brick" pattern
- Scissors
- Crayons
- Glue
- Colored Poster Board (or large sheet of chart paper)

TIME NEEDED

20 minutes

OBJECTIVE

The students will be able to see that in order to build our good character it is like two bricks being added to a foundation when we show good character and like taking one brick away when we make a mistake.

PROCEDURES

Give each student one worksheet page of "Brick" patterns. Students will be instructed to cut out the ten bricks on the worksheet. The leader should place the piece of poster board (or chart paper) at the front of the room.

Volunteers from the room will be asked to tell of a time when they were KIND to someone. The leader should call on one or two children to share their stories. Then each child can come to the front of the room and each glue two bricks (stacked) on the poster (it will be a total of 4 bricks if two children participated). Next, volunteers will be asked to share a time they were NOT kind to someone. The volunteer(s) will then tear off one brick.

This game will continue with the character actions of BEING TRUTHFUL (or telling a lie), SHARING (or being selfish), etc.

After a long stack of bricks has "been built" the leader should say to the children:

"Do you see how the wall kept going up even though some mistakes were made? It's the same way with our acts of good character. We want to keep trying to do the right thing even if we make some mistakes along the way!"

FOLLOW-UP QUESTIONS

1. Have you ever been really sorry for being unkind to someone or telling a lie? How did you feel?

2. When you are nice or kind to someone or you tell the truth to someone, how do you feel?

3. Which kind of character do you want to build on - good character with pleasant feelings or bad character with unpleasant feelings? Why?

OPTIONAL ENDINGS

K-2 The leader could begin to notice when children exhibit good character traits and stack two blocks on a table at the front of the room. When someone makes a mistake (for example, pushes or shoves in line) the leader could take a block off. When 4 stacks (or sides of a house) are completed with 10 blocks each, the class could "celebrate" their good character traits with an extra recess!

3-5 Students could be label each brick with a good character trait or act as it is added to their "house". The good character houses could then be displayed in the school media center or lunchroom for all students to see!

Activity 3:
Brick Pattern

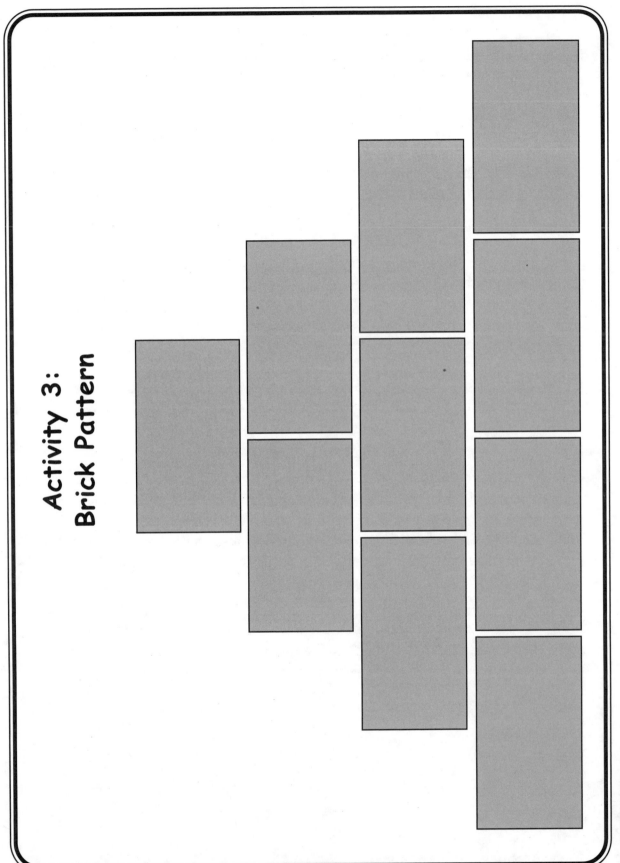

CHOOSING YOUR BUILDING SITE

Keys to CHOICES

 Your character is your choice.

 Your good character is something that can never be taken away from you unless you make the choice to change it.

 Good choices are available to everyone.

 We need to make good choices BEFORE we ACT.

 Your attitude is your choice.

 Remember - the SUCCESSFUL ATTITUDE is the POSITIVE ATTITUDE.

 Make a choice to DO YOUR BEST.

 If you hear someone talking bad about someone else, make a choice not to listen (just walk away).

 Make a choice to stay away from those who use bad language.

 Choose to stay away from all drugs!

 Make a choice to develop good posture habits.

 Proper exercise improves health and character stamina.

 Choose to set goals - both short and long term.

 Make a choice to enjoy and improve at least one of your hobbies.

 Good character is found in good literature - make a choice to READ more.

(Sample Parent Letter)

Dear Parent(s)/Guardian(s):

We will be discussing good and bad choices for the next several days. Some of these choices involve our own actions - such as telling the truth, being kind to others, following rules, choosing good friends, and others.

Please encourage your child to discuss these lessons with you. Ask your child:

1) Did you have to make any hard choices today? What choice did you make?

2) Tell me a good choice you made at school today.

3) Tell me a poor choice you made and let's talk about how you can make a better choice next time.

PRAISE your child at home when he/she makes good choices. Some examples would be when homework is done promptly, when chores are done without being reminded, when good manners are shown, when your child walks away from an argument with a brother or sister so they won't fight, etc.

Thanks for your participation!

Sincerely,

Activity 4:
CHAIN OF CHOICES!

BRIEF OVERVIEW

This lesson stresses the importance of good daily choices. The use of a chain is a good visual reminder that can be displayed in the classroom.

MATERIALS NEEDED

- Scissors
- Glue
- Colored construction paper (various colors would be nice!)
- "Chain of Choices" worksheet (1 per student)

TIME NEEDED

20-25 minutes

OBJECTIVE

Students will be able to recognize the choices that are available to them every day.

PROCEDURES

The worksheet found on page 18 contains sentence strips with the following:

I can make a choice to be nice!
I can make a choice to share!
I can make a choice to tell the truth!
I can make a choice to do my best!
I can make a choice to smile!

Lead the class in a discussion of these sentences. Students will notice that small, daily good choices are needed to have good, pleasant days!

Next students will be asked to make a chain by cutting out the six strips and gluing 5 of them. With the one left, one child will join his/her chain to the child on his/her right. Then the child on the right will find another child to join chains with, etc. until the entire class has completed a class character chain full of good choices!

This can be displayed in the room and serve as a reminder of good choices every day!

FOLLOW-UP QUESTIONS

1. How old do you have to be to make good choices? Are you old enough now?

2. What are some other choices you are allowed to make almost every day?

3. What are some choices you may have to make as you get older?

OPTIONAL ENDINGS

K-2 Students could take each chain home and discuss making good choices with their families.

3-5 Two or three blank sentence strips (the same size as those on the work sheet) could be given to each child. After the "Follow-up Questions" have been discussed, each child could write two or three good choices they can make (in addition to those provided on the worksheet). These can be added to the individual or classroom chains!

Activity 4:
CHAIN OF CHOICES! Worksheet

I can make a choice to be nice!

I can make a choice to share!

I can make a choice to tell the truth!

I can make a choice to do my best!

I can make a choice to smile!

18

Activity 5:
RIGHT or WRONG?

BRIEF OVERVIEW

This lesson is done in a game format where all children in the class are allowed to participate and all children can be winners! Even the rules of the game are viewed as "important choices", consequences for their actions are reinforced, and are included in the fun!

MATERIALS NEEDED

- "RIGHT or WRONG" worksheet
- 1 "RIGHT" sign (big lettering-5"+)
- 1 "WRONG" sign (big lettering-5"+)

TIME NEEDED

15 minutes

OBJECTIVE

Each student will think about, choose, and remember the good and bad choices available constantly.

PROCEDURES

Place the "RIGHT" sign on one side the room (or playground). The "WRONG" sign will be on the other side. The children should stand at the back of the room (or playground) in a neutral area.

The rules of the game are as follows(except for emergencies, of course):
1) No talking.
2) No raising hands.
3) No arguing.

The leader should explain the "RIGHT" sign is for the "RIGHT" choice and the "WRONG" sign is for the "WRONG" choice. When the leader reads a statement (from the "RIGHT" or "WRONG" worksheet, each child will make a choice to either go to the "RIGHT" sign or the "WRONG" sign. If they talk, raise their hands, or argue they are out of the game for the next choice (then they may return after having stayed in the neutral area for one turn).

After all statements have been completed, the class should be praised for the way each child improved on making better or "RIGHT" choices. Then, a discussion should follow using the "FOLLOW-UP" questions.

FOLLOW-UP QUESTIONS

1. Raise your hand if you can tell me when it was hard to make the "RIGHT" choice.

2. Tell me some choices you have to make in our classroom.

3. Tell me some choices you have to make on our playground or lunchroom.

4. What choices are hardest to make at home (for example, sharing with a brother, doing your chores, etc.).

OPTIONAL ENDINGS

K-2: The leader can write some of the difficult choices the children say they must make at school on a large piece of chart paper. When the child is noticed making a good choice in one of those areas over the following week (or longer), the child's name could be placed under the "RIGHT" sign at the front of the room. At the end of that week, the principal or another adult could be called in to really praise those children who have made "RIGHT" choices!

3-5: Allow the children to tell some other "RIGHT" or "WRONG" choices they have had to make in the last several weeks. This could be done orally, or as an individual or group writing assignment and posted on a bulletin board!

Activity 5:
"RIGHT" or "WRONG" Statements

*It is important that each statement is discussed after children have chosen RIGHT or WRONG!

1. Someone pushes you when lining up for lunch. You should push back! (WRONG)

2. You push someone down on the playground accidentally. You should stop, tell them you are sorry, and help them get up. (RIGHT)

3. Your leader is giving a test. You should look on your friend's paper if you don't know the answer. (WRONG)

4. On the playground someone calls you a bad name. You should walk away or look the other way if possible. (RIGHT)

5. In the classroom, you should listen carefully to your leader. (RIGHT)

6. When someone else is talking, but you have something to say, you should just talk louder so you can be heard! (WRONG)

7. If you get mad, you should walk away to cool down or go talk to a leader or some adult who will listen. (RIGHT)

8. If you get mad, you should hit someone. (WRONG-NEVER!)

9. On the bus, you should stand in your seat if you can't see well. (WRONG)

10. If you know that someone plans to hurt another person, you should ALWAYS tell your leader or another adult. (RIGHT)

11. When one of your crayons or your pencils breaks, you should grab someone else's. (WRONG)

12. If someone threatens to hurt you, you should report this to an adult immediately! (RIGHT)

13. When you don't understand what the leader is teaching, you should raise your hand and ask for more help. (RIGHT)

14. In the lunchroom, you should exchange food with friends. (WRONG)

15. It is important to say PLEASE or THANK YOU. (RIGHT)

16. If we can't say something nice about another person, then we shouldn't say anything at all. (RIGHT)

17. When we run in the hall, it is OK as long as no one sees us! (WRONG)

18. We should draw in class if we aren't interested in the lesson. (WRONG)

19. If we are wrong in the way we act, we need to admit it and say we are sorry. (RIGHT)

20. We should try harder next time, if we make a mistake. (RIGHT)

21. If someone trips and falls down, we should laugh and make fun of them. (WRONG)

22. When someone else does not have enough paper in their desk, we should share if we have extra paper. (RIGHT)

23. If there is a bully on the playground who is picking at another child, we should help the bully out so he/she won't pick at us! (WRONG)

24. If someone touches a private place on our bodies we should tell our parents, our leader, our school counselor, or some adult immediately. (RIGHT)

25. We should practice waiting for our turn on the playground. (RIGHT)

26. If the leader doesn't call on us when we raise our hand, we should just shout the answer out. (WRONG)

27. If we feel the leader has not been fair, it's OK to talk with the leader, in private, so maybe we can understand how to improve our relationship. (RIGHT)

28. School can be more fun when the rules are followed by everyone! (RIGHT)

29. Good character means making good choices. (RIGHT)

30. Good character means having a good attitude. (RIGHT)

Congratulations! We have a class who is learning RIGHT from WRONG! We can be examples to other classes in our school. Thank You All!

Activity 6:
FRIENDS WITH CHARACTER!

BRIEF OVERVIEW

Children can realize and become aware that peers they choose to play with influences their own behaviors(s). Also, when children model good behavior for others, sometimes others will choose better character!

MATERIALS NEEDED

- "Friends With Character!" poem on page 25
- 2 puppets (any kind of animal or people will work)

TIME NEEDED

15-20 minutes

OBJECTIVE

The students will learn the importance of choosing positive friends.

PROCEDURES

Introduce each puppet. One is "Good Choice Gerry" and the other is "Poor Choice Polly". The puppets will engage in a conversation about choosing friends. The story can go as follows (or the leader may adapt to situations that may arise within the class):

Good Choice Gerry says, "I love this school year. I have made so many new friends!"

Poor Choice Polly says, "Well no one likes me and I don't know why."

Good Choice Gerry says, "Have you been kind and nice to everyone?"

Poor Choice Polly says, "I really am not sure. When no one speaks to me I tell them things that really aren't true to get their attention."

Good Choice Gerry	says, "Well that's telling a lie! Don't you see that no one wants to be friends with anyone who tells a lie?"
Poor Choice Polly	says, "Well how do I get others to speak to me?"
Good Choice Gerry	says, "You can always smile and say something kind - like tell them you like their smile or offer to share a toy with them. It works for me!"
Poor Choice Polly	says, "Will you help me?"
Good Choice Gerry	says, "Sure, that's the first <u>good</u> choice I've heard you make!"

FOLLOW-UP QUESTIONS

1. What are some more poor choices you have made when trying to be a friend to others? How can you make better choices?

2. What can you do when you see your friend making poor choices? What will you do if your friend doesn't want to make better choices?

3. Let's agree to help each other in our class make better choices. How can we do that as a class?

OPTIONAL ENDINGS

K-2: Play the taped song "Friends are Friends Forever" as the class has quiet time.

3-5: When the leader notices friends arguing during class, offer a "cool down" time and then discuss what poor character choices caused the argument and what better character choices could have prevented it!

FRIENDS WITH CHARACTER!

All of us want many friends,
But sometimes I must know
That the friends I have must help me
As I learn and grow!

If Meg is **kind** and **shares** with me
Then I can laugh and play
But, if she chooses to push or shove
Then I must walk away!

If Hal is very **honest**
And tells the **truth** every time,
Then I can **trust** his friendship
No matter-rain or shine!

If I make a really poor choice
And no one wants to play
Then I must understand
To try harder the next day!

Good choices are more important
To each and every one
And, even though I make mistakes
I can change and have more fun!

Each and every day at school
As I learn and play
I want to choose good friends
And BE ONE every day!

Character Under Construction

CLEARING THE LAND FOR RESPONSIBLE BUILDING!

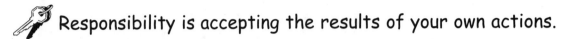 Keys to RESPONSIBILITY

 Responsibility is accepting the results of your own actions.

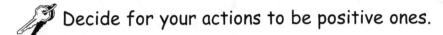 You are only responsible for yourself.

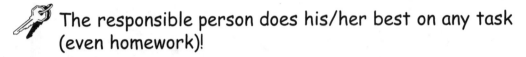 Decide for your actions to be positive ones.

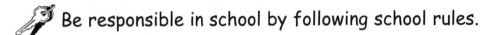 The responsible person does his/her best on any task (even homework)!

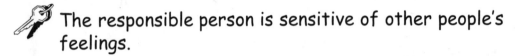 Be responsible in school by following school rules.

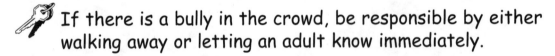 The responsible person is sensitive of other people's feelings.

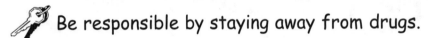 If there is a bully in the crowd, be responsible by either walking away or letting an adult know immediately.

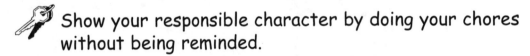 Be responsible by staying away from drugs.

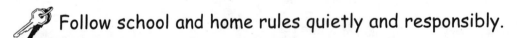 Show your responsible character by doing your chores without being reminded.

Follow school and home rules quietly and responsibly.

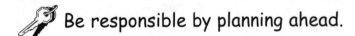 If you have a pet, be responsible for feeding and giving it water daily.

Be responsible by planning ahead.

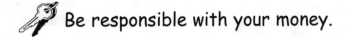 When you show a responsible attitude, most adults will trust you to do more on your own.

Be responsible with your money.

© 2000 YouthLight, Inc.

Clearing The Land For Responsible Building!

(Sample Parent Letter)

Dear Parent(s)/Guardian(s):

For the next several lessons in our Character Education series, we will be discussing the meaning of "RESPONSIBIL-ITY" - at home, school, and our world! In simple terms, we will recognize that this means doing our part to make our world a better place!

Please be prepared to listen as your child shares the lessons. As the parent, you need to share some of your responsibilities around your home and your responsibilities to care for your family and friends. Help your child formulate thought patterns that show why responsibility is so impor-tant in the life of each person - both young and old!

Thanks again for your participation in combining this pro-gram both at home and school. It is such an important growth tool for your child's preparation for the future!

Sincerely,

Activity 7:
RESPONSIBLE RACHEL!

BRIEF OVERVIEW

Younger children need to be able to relate their lives to the concept of responsibility. The short story which is a part of this lesson does just that! Creative thinking and actual responsibilities are enhanced through this activity.

MATERIALS NEEDED
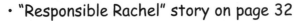
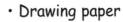
- "Responsible Rachel" story on page 32
- Drawing paper
- Crayons or colored pencils

TIME NEEDED

20-25 minutes

OBJECTIVES

Students will be able to name and re-think their own responsibilities. Students will be able to identify one new chore they can begin to complete.

PROCEDURES

Begin by briefly explaining the word - RESPONSIBILITY - to the children. The leader would stress that all people - young and old - have responsibilities.

Next, the leader should read the story, "Responsible Rachel!" to the children. When the story is over, the children should be allowed to express their reactions to the story.

A discussion should then follow with each child naming at least one or two responsibilities they have either at home or in school (the leader could list these on the board).

Finally, children should be given a sheet of drawing paper, crayons, or colored pencils and be asked to draw themselves actively completing the chore (or chores) for which they are responsible.

FOLLOW-UP QUESTIONS

1. When is the best time to do your chores? Would it help to choose the same time every day or just do these chores as you think about it?

2. Name some chores your parent(s)/guardian(s) have each day.

3. Name some chores your leader(s) have each day.

OPTIONAL ENDINGS

K-2 Think of one new chore you can begin to do at home or school on your own!

3-5 Make a "Responsibility Chart" and take it home to put on the refrigerator or in your room as a reminder?

All grade levels can take the drawings and any captions to put on a bulletin board with the "Responsible Rachel" story posted in the middle of the display.

RESPONSIBLE RACHEL!

Rachel was 5 years old and loved to play outside! One day, Rachel's mom asked her to take out the garbage. Rachel said that she would-IN JUST A MINUTE. Well, Rachel got busy playing ball with her puppy and forgot. That night, Rachel's mom called out, "Rachel, I believe you forgot to take out the garbage. What have I told you about being responsible?" Rachel felt really bad and promised it would never happen again.

The next day Rachel and her mom were going to the store. Rachel's mom told Rachel to pick up her toys before they left. Rachel said she would-IN JUST A MINUTE. Rachel got busy playing with her dolls and then went to the store, forgetting to pick up her toys. When they returned from the store, Rachel's mom was bringing in some bags and fell over a toy in the middle of the den. "Rachel!" her mom cried out, "I thought you were going to pick up your toys before we left for the store! What have I told you about being responsible?" Rachel felt really bad and promised it would never happen again.

That morning Rachel asked her mom if they could have pizza for lunch (she loved pizza). Mom said,"Sure!" However, about an hour later when Rachel realized it was time for lunch and went into the kitchen there was NO mom and NO pizza. Puzzled, Rachel began to look around the house and found her mom washing a window in her bedroom. Rachel said, "Mom, I thought I asked for pizza at lunch and you said okay?" "Rachel," mom asked, "What if I forgot our lunch like you forgot your chores? What if I was not responsible? How would you feel?" (Pause)

Rachel suddenly understood all about RESPONSIBILITY and the importance of keeping up with her chores! "Mom," said Rachel, " I really will try much harder. I am really sorry. From now on you will know me as RESPONSIBLE RACHEL!"

Mom looked at Rachel and smiled. "Rachel, let's go cook our pizza together! We'll both agree to be responsible for our own chores!"

Activity 8:
"ROCKIN' RESPONSIBILITY"

BRIEF OVERVIEW

Children can realize that responsibility for our world depends on each of us accepting our part-whether directly or indirectly. The song "Rockin' Responsibility" is sung to the tune of "Pop Goes the Weasel" as a fun and simple reminder to children of responsibilities at school, home, and everywhere!

MATERIALS NEEDED

- "Rockin' Responsibility" lyrics
- Dictionary(or written definition of Responsibility on the board)

TIME NEEDED

20 minutes

OBJECTIVES

Students will identify and name specific responsibilities at school and home. Students will be able to define the term "responsibility".

PROCEDURES

Introduce the lesson by explaining the definition of responsibility. On the board list various responsibilities that the children have at school (i.e. having a pencil sharpened, having paper at their desks, putting up supplies after an activity, etc.). Then, list responsibilities or chores they might have at home (i.e. taking out trash, feeding a pet, etc.). Finally, ask them to name some of the responsibilities of the leader or their parent(s) and list these on the board.

Ask the students what would happen if they decided not to take responsibility at school. What would our class be like? What if you did not do your chores at home? What if the leader or your parent(s)/guardian(s) did not accept responsibility at home or on the job?

Now, have the students stand and begin to have them sing "Rockin' Responsibility." Learn one verse at a time. This may be learned from memory by practicing several mornings consecutively as a reminder of responsibilities!

FOLLOW-UP QUESTIONS

1. What responsibilities do you have that are the most fun?

2. What responsibilities do you have that are the hardest to do?

3. What responsibilities do you wish your leader or parents would let you do? When do you think you will be able to do these things?

OPTIONAL ENDINGS

K-2: Assign daily responsibilities to groups of 2 or 3 students each. Some examples could be that one group clean the counter tops at the end of the day, one group could dust the desktops, one group could clean the board, etc.

3-5: Ask the class to decide on a "school responsibility" that could be done weekly for several weeks with each member participating. An example would be "playground cleanup" or helping maintain a portion of the outside landscape of the school.

ROCKIN' RESPONSIBILITY

(Sung to the tune of "Pop Goes the Weasel")

Responsibility is mine,
In many times and places.
I must do all my chores on time
TO SEE SMILING FACES!

Homework is the first on my mind.
At home I'd rather play.
But when I get it all done right,
I HAVE A BETTER DAY!

Next is the problem of making my bed.
It seems so unnecessary!
But when my room is tidy and neat,
IT LOOKS SO NICE AND AIRY!

Chores, chores, and chores some more.
It seems like they never end.
But even my mom and teacher have chores,
AND SO DO MY FRIENDS!

So there is no need to complain.
We all must do our part.
Responsibility is real
AND NEEDS TO COME FROM OUR HEART!
RESPONSIBILITY

Activity 9:
RACING RESPONSIBILITY!

BRIEF OVERVIEW

When tasks, chores, or any responsibility is completed on time, the first time, it allows the person who completes the responsibility more leisure time. Also, we all feel better about ourselves when we have done the best we can and fulfilled our responsibilities!

MATERIALS NEEDED

- Race Car Worksheet on page 38
- Crayons or colored pencils

TIME NEEDED

15 minutes

OBJECTIVE

Each student will identify the positive results of handling responsibility before fun activities.

PROCEDURES

Mention one responsibility and point to a student. That student should answer, "I'LL DO IT TOMORROW!" Use the following statements (or ones to fit your class):

LEADER Please clean up the water by the drinking fountain.

STUDENT I'LL DO IT TOMORROW!

LEADER Please turn in your Math worksheet.

STUDENT I'LL DO IT TOMORROW!

LEADER Please erase the board for me.

STUDENT I'LL DO IT TOMORROW!

LEADER Please wash your hands so you can eat your lunch.

STUDENT (The class will probably laugh here!)

Point out that even though some chores aren't the most fun, they are necessary and our responsibility. Now, change the student statement above to

"SURE, I'LL BE GLAD TO!" The leader should restate the leader parts and have different students respond with the more positive, cheerful response.

Ask the class to think about how they felt with the more positive responses. What happens when we put things off until tomorrow (or a later date)? Does this ever make you feel bad or cause someone to get upset with you? Do you sometimes forget a responsibility when you put it off until a later time?

What happens if you complete your work or chore immediately? How do you feel when it's done? Do you have more time to play when you finish your chores or work quickly? How does your teacher or parent react when you complete your work on time?

We are going to color a race car and underneath the car you can write a responsibility that you promise to complete on time every time!

FOLLOW-UP QUESTIONS

1. Who are some friends that you know who are very responsible?

2. Why do you think of them as responsible?

3. How do you think other people will feel when you start completing your responsibilities on time?

4. How will you feel about yourself when you've completed your responsibilities on time?

OPTIONAL ENDINGS

K-2: Copy additional "Race Car" worksheets. Each time a student improves on completing his/her responsibility on time, the leader should fill in the statement below the car and hang it in front of the classroom (or send home for a parent to see).

3-5: At the end of each school day (about 5 minutes) for the following week, ask each student to share with the class one responsibility that they are completing faster since our "Race Car" lesson!

Activity 9:
RACE CAR Worksheet

_____

_____

_____

_____

_____

_____

CHOOSING A KIND BUILDER !

Keys to KINDNESS

 Be kind to yourself.

 Be kind to others.

 Remember - being kind at all times to all people never hurts.

 Being kind includes choosing only nice words to leave you mouth.

 Be kind to those around you having a "sad day".

 Be kind and polite - even when everyone around you seems to be in a hurry.

 Sometimes the kindest action is a silent action.

 Small acts of kindness are important!

 K - I - N - D = Kindness Insures that Nice Deeds are done!

 Kind thoughts lead to kind actions.

 Kind actions cause kind reactions!

 A smile (or a kind expression on our face) - even during the worst of times - encourages others!

 When you are kind to others, you feel better about yourself.

 The kindness in your heart helps make peacefulness in your mind.

 A kind face shows natural beauty.

 Always show kindness toward senior citizens or older people.

 Kind deeds SHOULD be returned.

Choosing A Kind Builder!

(Sample Parent Letter)

Dear Parent(s)/Guardian(s):

During the next week we will be talking about different KIND actions we can show toward others. This is part of the Character Education lessons we are doing throughout the school year.

Our activities may include completing a class collage of pictures and learning a little "rap" call the "KIND FIND RAP!" That should be fun! We may decide to perform this for other classes!

Your participation in these activities is greatly needed! First, our class needs old magazines so we can cut out pictures. Secondly, I am enclosing copies of the "KIND FIND RAP!" If you could, please practice this with your child beginning today!

Praise your child when a kind action is done by them without being told! Remind them how proud you are of their good character development!

Thanks!

Sincerely,

Activity 10:
KIND KOLLAGE

BRIEF OVERVIEW

This activity is wonderful for a Friday afternoon or rainy day fun project. Acts of kindness will be apparent in all kinds of situations and places. The collage will make a wonderful display and serve as a reminder that acts of kindness can and do occur everywhere!

MATERIALS NEEDED

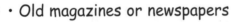

- Glue
- Scissors
- Pictures(that can be cut and pasted)
- Old magazines or newspapers
- Bulletin Board paper (as large or small as desired)

TIME NEEDED

20-30 minutes

OBJECTIVE

Visual, auditory, and kinesthetic students will participate in learning various acts of kindness that occur in different places and situations.

PROCEDURES

Explain that acts of kindness can and do occur at any time and in any place. First, the students will brainstorm and share something or someone who has shown them an act of kindness recently. (The leader should note these on the border of the Bulletin Board paper.) Next, the leader should be prepared to share some specific acts of kindness he/she has seen by students in the school at various times and in different places. (These should be included on the Bulletin Board paper, also.)

Finally, divide the class into groups of 2 or 3 students and provide each small group with drawing paper, glue, scissors, and old magazines (or newspapers) that can be cut apart. Have the students search for pictures of people (or animals) providing acts of kindness for others. Once these are cut out, let the students arrange and glue the pictures on the group's piece of Bulletin Board paper.

Display the students' creations either in the room or outside of the room for all the school to view!

FOLLOW-UP QUESTIONS

1. Think about some acts of kindness we have discussed and seen in the pictures. Decide how you can provide more acts of kindness at school, on the bus, on the playground, and at home.

2. When can you offer acts of kindness that are the most unexpected?

3. When someone is mean to you, how can an act of kindness in return help make things better?

OPTIONAL ENDINGS

K-2: If parents have participated in sending old magazines for the pictures to be cut out, your class may choose to complete "individual" collages on colored construction paper-rather than a class project.

3-5: Each child could choose 3-5 pictures to glue on a piece of construction paper and then draw a picture of their own showing an act of kindness. They may even wish to write about the picture!

You may wish to post in the Teacher's Lounge or send home with Parent Letter.

WANTED !!!

Old magazines or children's picture books that

may be cut up. These will not be returned,

but will be used for a class project on KINDNESS!

Please give to

_____
(name)

by _____
(date)

Thanks so much!!

44

Activity 11:
KIND FIND RAP!

BRIEF OVERVIEW

The message found in the rap is designed to help young children notice small acts of kindness. The rap is written from the viewpoint of an elementary student and is easy for the primary grade child to understand and learn kind actions. Also, children in grades 4-6 can learn and perform this rap for the younger children!

MATERIALS NEEDED

- Large chart paper (or poster board)
- "KIND FIND RAP!"

TIME NEEDED

20 minutes

OBJECTIVES

Each student will become aware of opportunities to consistently offer kind deeds to others. The student will become more proactive (rather that reactive) with kind actions.

PROCEDURES

Discuss kind actions that are available consistently at school, home, in stores, etc. The leader should point out that being kind has great rewards such as making more friends, keeping their surroundings more safe, staying out of trouble, etc.!

The "KIND FIND RAP!" (found on page 47) will be lead by the leader with the class clapping their hands to the rhythm. This should be displayed in the front of the classroom on large chart paper or poster board. Talk about the words and meaning of the rap as the students learn it. Gradually have the class learn verse by verse until everyone participates!

Practice the rap each morning as a "kindness" reminder activity. When the class learns it, have them perform and explain it to another class within the school!

FOLLOW-UP QUESTIONS

1. Am I a "Kind Find Chap"? If not, how can I become one?

2. What are some opportunities I have to be kind that are not found in this rap?

3. Who has been a really kind person in my life? Have I ever thanked them for their kindness?

OPTIONAL ENDINGS

K-2: 1. Students could perform this before parents at an open house or a special occasion with a narrator from the class explaining some of the acts of kindness the students have learned from this lesson!

2. Have each student name and draw a picture of the KIND FIND CHAP and display around the poster which displays the rap.

3-5: 1. In groups, students could attempt to write and title their own "KIND" rap. These could be performed by each group in front of other classmembers.

2. Send some of the original raps to the school newspaper (or design a "Kindness Flyer") to be read by all students in the school.

"KIND FIND RAP"

Let me tell ya' about a really cool chap.
He's the person in this Kind Find Rap!
He comes to our school each and every day
And decides to be Kind all the way!

Now, when someone pushes him in line
He flashes his smile until his teeth shine.
Now, who can fuss at this act of kind,
Because that smile stays right in your mind!

Then, when he goes into the classroom
And faces show some morning doom,
The Kind Find Chap will begin to greet
Each and every other child he meets!

Now, as the teacher holds a flashcard
And says, "Now, class, let's try real hard."
The Kind Find Chap gives all he's got
To learn his best and forward trot......

To the playground equipment he does climb,
To play and show the girls he's fine!
But, if it is another's turn,
He moves aside just as he's learned!

Since you know good character counts,
Just practice kind acts and they will mount!
Now, you too can be a Kind Find Chap.
Just remember this special Kind Find Rap!

Activity 12:
KINDNESS CORNERS!

BRIEF OVERVIEW

This lesson will help younger children think of different ways to show kind actions in various settings every day. It will encourage them to begin to think of others more!

MATERIALS NEEDED

- Index cards
- 4 (2'X2') pieces of paper or poster board

TIME NEEDED

30 minutes

OBJECTIVE

Students will recognize and practice kind actions in various settings.

PROCEDURES

In each corner of the classroom will be a sign (2'X2'). The following will be printed on each sign:

1) CLASSROOM   3) BUS
2) HOME   4) STORE

One index card will be made for each student to draw out of a basket. (The leader should make an even number of each of the above places. For example, if there are 20 students there would be 5 cards each with 1 of the 4 places on each card.)

Instruct the students to draw a card and go to the matching corner. Each corner group will then think of 5 ways to show kindness in that place. Give them 5-8 minutes for this activity.

For home, examples could be: 1) Take mom a flower from the yard when she is tired; 2) Take dad a drink of water when he's outside working; etc.

Bring the class back together at the end of this activity. Have each group stand before the class and report the KIND actions decided on together.

After each group shares have the remainder of class to give several additional ideas.

Challenge the class to be the KINDEST CLASS AT OUR SCHOOL!

FOLLOW-UP QUESTIONS

1. Where, do you feel, is it the hardest place to be kind-the classroom, home, bus, or store? Why?

2. Where do you see others being the kindest-the classroom, home, bus, or store? What about the place people are the most UNKIND? Why do you think this happens?

3. List some other places we can practice our kind actions.

OPTIONAL ENDINGS

K-2: The leader could write the actions each group discussed and copy these for the students to take home and discuss with parents! Ask the students to be "tattle tales"! Tell them to TELL on any person they notice DOING one of the KIND actions discussed today!

Keys to MANNERS

 Good manners exhibit good character choices.

 Use good manners at school - in the halls, lunchroom and school grounds, as well as the classroom.

 Use good manners at home.

 If someone else has bad manners at your table, ignore them. If that doesn't work, ask them to "Please stop."

 Always choose to speak in polite ways.

 When in busy lines always remember to say "EXCUSE ME" if you need to get through to another area.

 Let others finish talking before you begin speaking.

 Speak as clearly as possible.

 Speak calmly in order to get the best results when you are upset.

 When an adult is walking through a door, always stand aside and let the adult go first.

 Remember - in most public places it is best to remove your cap or hat when indoors.

Mannerly Workers Needed!

(Sample Parent Letter)

Dear Parent(s)/Guardian(s):

Our Character Education lessons for the next couple of weeks will focus on "Good Manners" at home, school, and everywhere. We will be learning and practicing proper table manners, proper speaking manners (PLEASE, THANK YOU, YOU ARE WELCOME, EXCUSE ME, etc.) and the importance of proper voice tone (speaking calmly and softly, rather than in loud tones).

Please encourage your child to practice and talk about these lessons at home, as well as at school. We are stressing how our world becomes more pleasant as good manners are practiced - both young and old.

There is a poem, "Good Manners Every Day", that we are challenging each child to memorize for a special award! Please help your child if he or she asks!

Here's more to GOOD MANNERS! Thank you!

Sincerely,

Activity 13:
TERRIFIC
TABLE MANNERS!

BRIEF OVERVIEW

In the world of children and adults, proper table manners make food more digestible and meals more pleasant. Children in the primary grades need to be taught what proper and basic table manners include. Follow-up PRACTICE during school lunches will improve manners and allow everyone at the table to enjoy lunch more!

MATERIALS NEEDED

- Worksheet with place setting and napkin
- Student scissors

TIME NEEDED

20-30 minutes

OBJECTIVE

Students will learn proper table manners.

PROCEDURES

Explain to students that our table manners are very important not only now, but as they grow up. Discuss certain good manners such as:

- Chewing your food with your mouth closed.
- Talking to others at your lunch table when you do not have food in your mouth(never talk with your mouth full!).
- Placing your napkin on your lap.
- Eating with one hand and keeping the other hand on your lap except when cutting food with a knife and fork combination, passing food to someone sitting beside you (never reach across the table), etc.
- Eating your salads (with the outside fork) and main entree next(with the inside fork).
- Using the napkin to wipe your mouth.

After this discussion with the students, have them cut out the pieces of the place setting from the worksheet on page 56. Have them practice setting the table properly (as shown) and placing the napkin on their lap. (While there are other ways of setting a more formal table, this is most common for general settings.)

When the children feel more comfortable with these table manners, have a leader-made chart ready with all student names included and 5 check-off days. Decide on a prize for the children exhibiting good table manners for the next 5 lunches (or 4 out of 5). Check these off daily and offer praise for the improved manners of the class!

FOLLOW-UP QUESTIONS

(After each lunch):

1. What did YOU do to improve your table manners today? (Do not allow children to discuss anyone but themselves!)

2. Did you notice the taste of your food more, less, or the same?

(After the 5 days):

1. Is it becoming easier to practice your good table manners after the last few days?
2. Where else will you be using these good table manners?

OPTIONAL ENDINGS

K-2: Ask the Principal or the Assistant Principal to observe the class once the table manners are beginning to improve. Ask this administrator to come in your class after lunch and praise the children for being so well mannered!

3-5: Plan a "manner meal" with paper plates and plastic forks and knives. Allow the children to invite a Kindergarten class. Let your class set the table, explain, and model good manners to the younger children!

Activity 13: Place Setting Worksheet

Activity 14:
VERA'S VOICE

BRIEF OVERVIEW

This lesson will point out the importance of voice tone when speaking to others. It is similar to the expression, "It's not what you say, but how you say it".

MATERIALS NEEDED

- Tape recorder
- Blank tape
- "Vera's Voice" story

TIME NEEDED

30 minutes

OBJECTIVES

Students will hear and recognize how the tone and pitch of our voices affect others. Students will develop better habits when speaking.

PROCEDURES

Before teaching this lesson tape voices in various settings (i.e. the school lunchroom, the playground, the classroom, etc.). When beginning the lesson the leader should model speaking softly to individual students and speaking very loud to the classroom when giving instructions. Ask the students:

1. Which voice did you like the best? Why?
2. Did I need to speak so loudly for you to hear?
3. When did you feel more comfortable: when I spoke loud or soft?
4. Why do you yell at others? Is it really necessary?

Today we are going to listen to a story about "Vera's Voice". At the end of the story, we will discuss how Vera can control her own voice to help others listen to her more.

FOLLOW-UP QUESTIONS

1. When are some times that you need to practice speaking in a softer, quieter voice?

2. When are some times that it is necessary to speak loudly or even yell?

3. How did the lesson today help you?

OPTIONAL ENDINGS

K-2: Bring a cartoon tape (approved through the school media center and administration) and play a 5 minute segment. Talk about the loud versus the soft voices of the characters and the differences it made in the communication.

3-5: Have several of your more "dramatic" children role play situations such as:

1) trying to get attention in the lunchroom at the table; or,

2) trying to get attention in the classroom, etc.

Be sure they role play the wrong way and the more MANNERLY and CORRECT way!

VERA'S VOICE

Every morning Vera rides to school on the bus. Her best friends, Sara and Tonya, sit together because they have to get on the bus before Vera. Sometimes they are talking when Vera gets on the bus so Vera will yell very loud to get their attention. If Sara and Tonya keep talking and ignore her, Vera's feelings get hurt.

One day Sara was sick and did not get on the bus. Vera got to sit with Tonya and said, "I wish I could sit with you every day. I never get to talk when Sara is on the bus." Tonya seemed surprised, "Well Vera, we would talk to you but you always YELL at us!" Vera was very surprised at that!

The next day Vera got on the bus and saw Sara. Instead of YELLING, Vera gave Sara and Tonya a picture she had drawn for them the night before. When they stopped to look at it, Vera said in a soft voice, "I hope you are feeling better Sara. We missed you. And thank you Tonya for telling me to stop YELLING. I never realized how I sounded to you. Can we still be friends? LEADER, lead the class in a discussion of the following questions.

1. Do you think Sara, Tonya and Vera are friends again?

2. How do you feel when people yell at you? Do you yell back? Does that help?

3. What would happen if we all yelled in this classroom to get attention?

4. When a teacher welcomes students each morning, how does her voice usually sound?

5. When you use good manners, what should your voice sound like (i.e. soft, medium, loud, etc.)?

6. Think of one time you can use a softer voice today. (i.e. On the school bus, in the school hall or classroom, at your family dinner table, next time you disagree with your sister or brother, etc.)

7. How do others react when you use a soft voice? A loud voice?

Activity 15:
MORE MANNERS!!!!

BRIEF OVERVIEW

This lesson shows how simple daily good manners are for all people. By reciting the poem found on page 62 and role playing/modeling good manners, children will internalize good manners that will become positive lifetime habits!

MATERIALS NEEDED

• "Good Manners Every Day" worksheet

TIME NEEDED

10-30 minutes*

* Depending on the depth of the Optional Ending chosen

OBJECTIVE

Students will become aware of good manner phrases (PLEASE, THANK YOU, YOU'RE WELCOME, EXCUSE ME, etc.)

PROCEDURES

The leader should model good manners and point out to the students that he/she practices good manners just as each student should on a daily basis. Ask the students to share some times that the terms PLEASE, THANK YOU, YOU'RE WELCOME, EXCUSE ME, etc. should be used. Point out that these good manners should be used at home, as well as in school and every place we go!

Read the poem "Good Manners Every Day" and tell the students to help you understand what the poem really is saying. After discussion, challenge the students to learn to recite this from memory (possibly offer an incentive to those who are able to memorize and say this after one week)!

FOLLOW-UP QUESTIONS

1. Tell me the difference between these two statements:

   "Give me your pencil NOW."
   OR
   "If you don't mind, could I PLEASE borrow your pencil?"

2. If someone accidentally pushes you down on the playground, what is the difference between these two sentences?

   "You should not have gotten in my way!"
   OR
   "EXCUSE ME, I really didn't mean to push you down."

3. As a class, how can we build our character and friendships by using these good manners that we have discussed today?

OPTIONAL ENDINGS

K-2: Ask the children to practice good manners as they go to their centers or work in cooperative groups. Recognize and praise children you notice using these good manners!

3-5: Teach children how to write simple "Thank You" notes!

GOOD MANNERS EVERY DAY!

Good manners are easy to do every day.
I simply must listen to what I say.
Saying PLEASE and THANK YOU is simple to do,
And shows good character, oh so true!
And when someone else says THANK YOU to me
I must remember to say YOU'RE WELCOME you see!

It doesn't matter if we are young or old,
We must be KIND to others and never cold.
Being KIND shows good manners in a special way,
By RESPECTING others each and every day.
Our manners are important to our self-esteem
And there is never, never room to be mean!

EXCUSE ME is a very important phrase
And will attract notice and probably praise!
Manners in all kinds of places
Include smiling and nodding to all kinds of faces.
I know that when good manners are shown
I will know that my character has really grown!

LAYING THE FOUNDATION WITH HONESTY!

🔑 Keys to HONESTY/INTEGRITY

🔑 Being honest shows others your good character.

🔑 Being truthful builds your own self-respect.

🔑 Being truthful takes courage.

🔑 Cheating is *not* being truthful. Remember - cheating eventually hurts you the most in many ways.

🔑 Being truthful helps keep us safe
(remember "The Boy Who Cried Wolf").

🔑 Being honest helps others respect you more.

🔑 Honesty is expected.

🔑 Honesty helps others to trust you more.

🔑 Honesty and integrity are parts of real friendships.

🔑 Honesty is for everyone.

🔑 Being honest is easy IF the truth is told the FIRST time.

🔑 When being honest use good manners - or tact.

🔑 You can be trusted when you are honest.

🔑 Honest actions build good character.

🔑 Honesty is to friendship as food is to the body.

Laying The Foundation With Honesty!

(Sample Parent Letter)

Dear Parent(s)/Guardian(s)):

In our Character Education lessons, we are currently discussing the importance of telling the truth and being honest! These lessons cover how we feel when we are not truthful through a story called "Miserable Millie" and also how our safety can be affected when the truth is not told through a poem called "Safety Sam".

Please notice the times your child is truthful when it is difficult and show how proud you are of his or her choice! Share with your child some time when you have had to be honest and it was a difficult situation. Allow your child to share with you the discussions we have in class about being honest.

Together, let's help our children understand this important character trait and its affect on both your life and that of your children!

Sincerely,

Activity 16:
MISERABLE MILLIE!

BRIEF OVERVIEW

This lesson will help students visualize the differences between TRUTH and LIES during a prepared story (found on page68) which requires student participation. The internal effects of "Cheating" will be noted. TRUTH will be enacted as simple and positive. LIES will be shown as complicated and negative.

MATERIALS NEEDED

- Blocks (NOTE: Large (3 in. or more) for K-1, Small (1-2 in.) for 2nd or 3rd grade)
- 2 pieces of construction paper (different colors)
- Magic marker
- Puppet (optional for K-1)

TIME NEEDED

20-30 minutes

OBJECTIVES

Students will recognize cheating behavior. Students will develop internal motivation for being honest with school assignments.

PROCEDURES

Tell the students that they are going to build one tower that will be weak and fall. Then, they will build one tower that will be strong and stand. When both towers have been built the students will be able to tell you what made the difference.

In the room have two piles of blocks-one will be the TRUTH pile and one will be the LIE pile. Label one piece of construction paper TRUTH and one piece of construction paper LIE. Put a sign behind each pile of blocks. Discuss the difference between telling the TRUTH and telling a LIE. Ask the children if they would like to share a story (about themselves, NOT another person) when telling the TRUTH helped them or when telling a LIE got them in trouble.

Next, explain to the class that you are going to read a story about telling the

TRUTH or telling LIES. Remind the students that you have a TRUTH pile of blocks and a LIE pile of blocks. Each time during the story that you say "BUILD IT!" you will point to a student who will then decide which tower should be constructed with one additional block.

Now begin reading the story, "MISERABLE MILLIE", found on the next page (if you choose the optional use of a puppet, use the puppet to read the story). Continue reading until the LIE tower falls or collapses. Discuss with the class how one little lie can lead to another little lie, and another, and another-until the person telling the lie is like the tower built on lies-the person falls (or gets caught)!

Last have the children look at the simple little TRUTH tower that is still standing! Note with the class how simple the truth is and how it still is standing very strong and tall!

FOLLOW-UP QUESTIONS

1. If Millie had told Ms. Smith she was sorry for drawing during morning work, how do you think Ms. Smith would have reacted?

2. If Millie had #5 wrong on the Spelling test, but knew in her heart that she had not copied, how would Millie have felt differently about herself?

3. Why did the TRUTH tower stay simple and small, but the LIE tower got bigger and bigger and fell down?

OPTIONAL ENDINGS

K-2: 1. Students could share ways that Millie can work on telling the truth so she will feel better about herself.

2. Students can talk about lessons Millie didn't learn because she was not telling the truth (so now she does not know how to spell the word she copied, or set the forks in the correct place, etc.).

3-5: 1. Students can write the ending to "If Millie had told the truth,…" as a journal entry.

2. Students can discuss (with the leader as the facilitator) the meaning of the word "cheating" and why cheating really hurts the person who is copying.

MISERABLE MILLIE!

Once upon a time at_____(name of your school) there were two children in _____(grade level you are teaching) grade who started their day at school feeling really happy! Together Millie and Shawn got off the bus and walked toward their classroom. As they entered the classroom, the teacher, Ms. Smith, gave them an assignment to begin for their morning work. Shawn listened carefully and began to work as Ms. Smith had asked. However, Millie liked to draw, so she got out a piece of paper and began drawing her dog. Ms. Smith said, "Class, is everyone working on their morning work?" Shawn nodded his head, "Yes" (BUILD IT!-TRUTH tower) and Millie nodded her head, "Yes" (BUILD IT!-LIE tower).

Ms. Smith began walking around the classroom. "Shawn, you are doing a really good job (BUILD IT!-TRUTH tower)! A child across the room raised her hand to ask a question and Ms. Smith went to help her. Millie realized all of a sudden that she had not done any of her morning work. Sitting next to Shawn, Millie looked at his work and began to copy it (BUILD IT!-LIE tower). As Millie quickly copied Shawn's answers and had almost caught up, Ms. Smith returned. Looking at Shawn's paper again, Ms. Smith helped him correct a mistake he had made while she was on the other side of the room.

Then, Ms. Smith looked at Millie's paper and noticed Millie had made the same mistake as Shawn! "Millie," Ms. Smith asked, "Are you working alone?" Millie looked down at the floor as she replied, "Yes, Ms. Smith." (BUILD IT!-LIE tower)

Ms. Smith looked surprised. Then Ms. Smith asked Millie to show her how she got the answer. Millie was afraid of telling the truth so she said, "Ms. Smith, I need a tissue" and Millie pretended to sneeze. (BUILD IT!-LIE tower) Ms. Smith agreed and began looking at the work from the other children.

Shawn got up to sharpen his pencil by the tissue box and said, "Millie, you were copying my paper." (BUILD IT!-TRUTH tower) "I was not!" Millie replied (BUILD IT!-LIE tower) "I never looked at your paper!" (BUILD IT!-LIE Tower) "I know all the answers because I listened to the teacher tell us how to do the work this morning!" (BUILD IT!-LIE tower)

Ms. Smith then asked Shawn and Millie to return to their desks. She began taking up the papers and talking to the class about the importance of always telling the truth. She said that truth helps you feel better inside yourself and you are able to learn more by truthfully asking questions when you don't understand something the teacher explained.

Feeling really bad inside, Millie thought to herself, "Oh, well I didn't get caught so it really doesn't matter." (BUILD IT!-LIE tower) She decided not to think about it anymore. The class was getting ready for a test in spelling. Millie got out her paper and pencil and remembered that she had not studied the night before! Ms. Smith called out the first four spelling words and Millie knew each of them. As she began to relax, Ms. Smith called out the 5th spelling word and Millie couldn't remember how to spell it! Millie looked at Shawn but his paper was covered! Then, she looked at Rashad's paper and could easily see how he had spelled the word. She quickly copied the word. (BUILD IT!-LIE Tower)

Suddenly, Ms. Smith shouted, "Millie what are you doing?" Millie said, "I don't know what you mean!" (BUILD IT!-LIE tower) Continuing, as if she had not heard Millie, Ms. Smith said, "Were you copying Rashad's paper?" "NO MA'AM!" Millie replied. (BUILD IT!-LIE tower) "Well keep your eyes on your own paper please," Ms. Smith said.

Millie felt awful inside. It seemed as if her day was getting worse! But, she chose not to tell the truth this time-AGAIN! After the spelling test, it would be a time in the cooking center with her friends. Things would probably get better there!

Later, Millie was at the cooking Center with Shawn, Rashad, Beverly, and Kim. They were going to practice setting the table and using good manners. Beverly offered to get the plates, Shawn and Kim offered to fold the napkins, and Millie was to help Rashad place the spoons, forks, and knives. But there was a problem! Yesterday, Millie was drawing when the teacher was telling the class how the spoons, forks, and knives had to be placed. Millie stood there while Rashad began with the spoons and knives. Millie said, "I don't want to place the forks. Ms. Smith didn't teach me the way my mom said to do it!" (BUILD IT-LIE tower)

*NOTE-If the blocks in the LIE tower haven't fallen, keep adding to the story with Millie's LIES until the tower collapses.

Activity 17:
DIGGING TOWARD TRUTHFUL CHARACTER!

BRIEF OVERVIEW

Even though it is difficult at times to tell the truth, this lesson offers choice and visuals to stress, that it's best tot ell the truth immediately!

MATERIALS NEEDED

- Green/Red Crayons
- "Shovel" worksheet

TIME NEEDED

20-30 minutes

OBJECTIVES

Each student will become aware of the importance of telling the truth the first time. Students will recognize the problems that result from lies.

PROCEDURES

Honesty will be defined as "TELLING THE TRUTH" to the students. Point out that telling the truth is not always easy at first, but it's the easiest way! Use the analogy of the student digging in the dirt. Tell the class to close their eyes and imagine each of them has a shovel in their hands. It's hard to get started but you find the first scoop of dirt is soft and easy to dig. The second scoop of dirt is harder to dig up. The third scoop of dirt gets even harder to get out of the hole. By the fourth scoop of dirt the shovel feels as if you have hit a ROCK, so you must stop or you will break your shovel! Have the students open their eyes.

Allow the class to talk about how telling the truth is like digging in the dirt at first. It may seem hard to get started, but it's really easy to do! If the truth is told the first time (while the dirt is soft), it's easier to accept the consequences. However, if a lie is told, then usually it takes another lie to cover up the first one, and it keeps going until you get caught and must stop (just like digging in the dirt until you hit the rock and the shovel might break)!

Give each class member a copy of the "Shovel" worksheet. Read the statements by each shovel to the class as they make a choice. They will color the shovel GREEN if the statement is TRUE or RED if the statement is FALSE. When completed, remind the class that the more they tell the truth, the easier it becomes! Have each student take the papers home to tell their families about the choices they have to always tell the truth, even when it's hard at first!

FOLLOW-UP QUESTIONS

1. If you know you may get into trouble if you tell the truth the first time, what will be the right choice? Why?

2. What will happen if you wait to tell the truth until someone "catches" you?

3. How will your family or teacher feel about you if they find out you have not been truthful? How will they feel if they know you always tell the truth?

OPTIONAL ENDINGS

K-2: A classroom book entitled We Dig for Truth can be compiled and stapled using all the completed "Shovel" worksheets and presented to the school library to be displayed.

3-5: A paragraph entitled We Dig for Truth can be written, with student drawings to display on the class bulletin board (or outside the classroom). DRAW "Shovel" WORKSHEET WITH TRUE/LIE STATEMENTS.

Activity 17: SHOVEL WORKSHEET

To be a friend, I must be kind.

It's OK to lie, if it is just a "little" one!

To be responsible means to do my chores without being remined.

To have courage means to be brave and make good choices.

Sharing is <u>not</u> for everyone.

We should respect others, but we don't always have to agree with them.

Good manners are only to be used with adults.

My homework is Mom's responsibility.

Good character is something I want to have <u>Now</u>!

Activity 18:
SAFETY SAM?

BRIEF OVERVIEW

Being honest sometimes means the difference between being safe or being in danger. This lesson will reinforce the importance of children telling the truth where there are rules to keep both themselves and others safe.

MATERIALS NEEDED

- Poem "Sam Breaks the Rules"
  * If you choose the optional endings, you may need 2"x8" strips of paper, glue, pencils, and/or markers.

TIME NEEDED

20-30 minutes

OBJECTIVES

Students will learn the reason the truth must be told when others are (or could be) in danger. Students will recognize the importance of the truth as related to the safety of themselves and others.

PROCEDURES

Explain to the class that telling the truth is very important in order to keep everyone safe! Use the example of your classroom rules. Go over those rules that pertain to the safety of the children (i.e. "Keeping hands and feet to themselves", etc.).

Tell the class you are going to read a poem about "Safety Sam?". As they prepare to listen, state that you will be asking questions at different times during the poem, so they must listen very carefully. Next, begin reading the poem and stop at the question points.

When the poem ends, summarize both the beginning class discussion and the poem. Stress the importance of always telling the truth-especially when safety issues are involved!

FOLLOW-UP QUESTIONS

1. If you realize you have broken a rule, what should you do if it could hurt someone or yourself?

2. If you disagree with a rule, who can you talk to about it?

3. What if I, as your counselor/teacher, decided to go very fast down the highway? Is that breaking a safety rule? Should I be punished? Should I tell the truth? Why?

OPTIONAL ENDINGS

K-2: On a chart or sentence strips, the counselor/teacher could write and display safety rules at each school or home or in general.

3-5: Give children strips of blank paper (2"X8"). Tell them to write a reason TRUTH must ALWAYS be told where rules are concerned. Make the strips into a chain and call it the "Safety Chain". Show the children what happens when one link is broken (like the one LIE that could break the "Safety Chain") and causes someone harm.

SAFETY SAM?

Rules, rules, everywhere-
    At home, at Scouts, and at school.
We even have rules
    At our swimming pool!

Now rules can be good
    As Sam will admit.
But some rules make Sam
    Want to throw a fit!

"Maybe," Sam thought,
    "Some rules can be bent."
So Sam began to interpret
What he thought they meant!

WHAT ARE SOME RULES THAT CAN BE DANGEROUS IF THEY ARE BENT?

Now, at home was the rule
    Toys must be picked up.
But at times Sam disagreed
    And blamed Mutt, the pup!

But Sam's dad walked through the den
    And fell over a toy crane.
Dad yelled and cried out
    In terrible pain!

WHAT SHOULD SAM DO NOW?

At Scouts Sam went on a camping trip
    And was setting up tent,
When he took Frank's medicine
    And put the blame on friend Brent!

Now, when Frank got very ill
    And the medicine couldn't be found

Sam was very, very upset
    But didn't utter a sound!

HOW IS THIS A LIE? WHAT COULD HAPPEN TO BRENT?

Running down the hall at school
    Sam continued to push and shove,
Until he reached his classroom
    As quick as a dove!

But on the way Sam knocked Kay down
    Sam fell too and cried out,
"I'm hurt and Kay did it!"
    Now she shouldn't pout!

WHAT LIE IS BEING TOLD? WHAT SCHOOL RULE WAS BROKEN?

Now, as summer approaches,
    Sam loved his swimming pool.
However, especially there,
    Sam must follow the rules.

But as Sam walks toward the
    Very tall ladder that leads to the slide,
He pushes and shoves to go first
    And down falls Clyde!

WHAT COULD HAPPEN HERE?

Now the lesson I hope that you all have learned,
    Is that telling the TRUTH is really cool,
And must be done
    With each and every rule!

This lesson is important and
    Is very easy to remember as you grow old.
Rules are made for your safety,
    AND THE TRUTH MUST ALWAYS BE TOLD!

TRUSTY TOOLS

🔑 Keys to TRUST

🔑 T - R - U - S - T = Trust equals Respect Under Serious Test!

🔑 Trust must be earned by practicing good character traits.

🔑 Trust is the quiet assurance between family and friends that "all is well" no matter what the circumstances.

🔑 Trust is believing that what is promised will really happen.

🔑 To break a promise for no good reason destroys trust.

🔑 Trust and faith go together - hand in hand.

🔑 Be able to trust yourself.

🔑 When your thoughts are pure and good, you can trust your actions to be pure and good.

🔑 Be trustworthy and others will trust you to handle more responsibilities.

🔑 Don't let one honest mistake by a friend destroy total trust.

🔑 Trust history to help you not repeat mistakes.

🔑 Trust the knowledge and advice of older people who love you.

🔑 Trust is needed everywhere!

Trusty Tools

(Sample Parent Letter)

Dear Parent(s)/Guardian(s):

TRUST is a character trait that we need in our adult worlds. This is sometimes a difficult concept for children to understand. While it is important for children to trust others, we want them to understand that we cannot trust everyone.

The lessons we will be having in our Character Education series will focus on the meaning of TRUST. We will be discussing the importance of trusting our own actions, keeping our own promises, as well as knowing when to trust others.

Also, we will be learning that "TRUST must be earned" and cannot be developed overnight!

Please allow your child to share our lessons and help your individual child begin to understand the concept of trust within your own home, as well as our school!

Thanks for your input and willingness to help your child grow in character!

Sincerely,

Activity 19:
"TRAIN"ING FOR TRUST

BRIEF OVERVIEW

Trust is important to each individual-both trust of oneself and trust of others. This lesson will explain the concept of trust to the children and discuss the factor of faith that must exist. This lesson brings in the good character trait of responsibility, too.

MATERIALS NEEDED

- "TRAIN" Worksheet
- Glue
- Scissors

TIME NEEDED

20-25 minutes

OBJECTIVES

The students will increase their vocabulary with words related to "TRUST". The students will recognize feelings when trust is present in a relationship.

PROCEDURES

Read from *180 Days of Character*, Day 90:

"When your thoughts are pure and good, you can trust your actions to be pure and good."

"• Allow only good thoughts to stay in your mind.
• When bad or mean thoughts keep coming in your mind talk them over with a parent, teacher, or school counselor.
• Good thoughts will bring kind and good actions."

Allow students to talk about each of these statements. Challenge them to think of a time when they were thinking a bad or mean thought. Ask, "What happened? How do you feel?" Then contrast that discussion by asking them to think of a good or nice thought. Ask, "What do you feel now? How would you act differently now?

Explain the meaning of TRUST as having faith. Explain that you really cannot see TRUST but you know it is there. For example:

1. When you come to school each day, you TRUST that there will be a teacher in your classroom with all kinds of activities planned for your day!

2. When you come to school each day, you TRUST that your principal and the teachers will take care of you until it is time to leave to go home.

Then, say, "You really aren't told either of these things each day that you come to school. You simply TRUST that you will have a teacher in the classroom and that your principal and teachers will take care of you!

Now, use the "TRAIN" worksheet on the following page. Have the children cut out the words related to TRUST and glue them on the train. Discuss the words as the children work. After the glue dries, have the children color the trains.

FOLLOW-UP QUESTIONS

1. Think of 2 people you trust the most. What makes you trust them?

2. How can you be trusted by other people like your parents or teacher?

3. We have studied "Responsibility". How can being "responsible" help others trust you more?

OPTIONAL ENDINGS

PreK-1: Each student could draw a picture of the person or people that he/she trusts the most.

2-3: In addition to drawing a picture of the person he/she trusts, a short story could be written to tell about the good character traits of that person (i.e. responsible, honest, etc.).

Activity 18: Train Worksheet

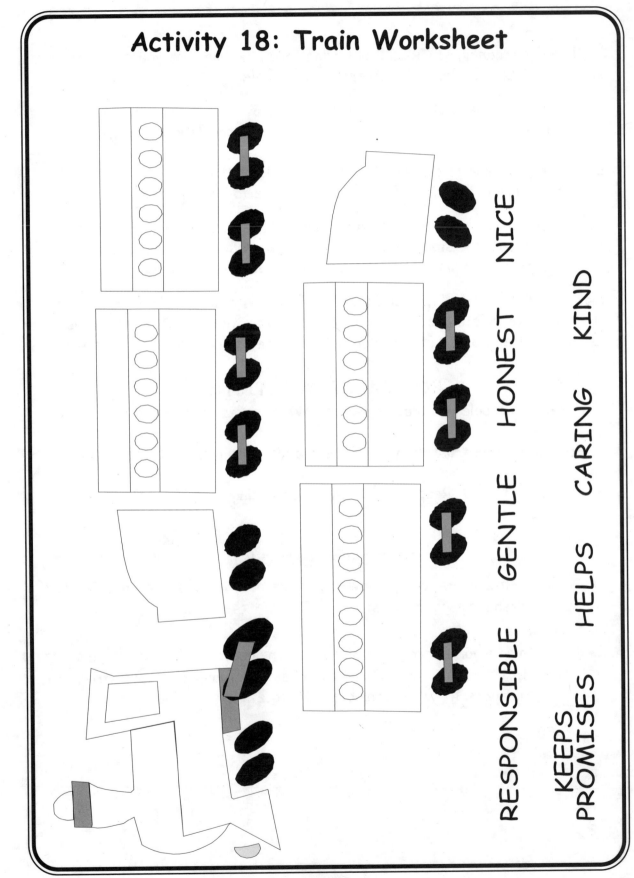

RESPONSIBLE GENTLE HONEST NICE

KEEPS PROMISES HELPS CARING KIND

Activity 20:
TRUST OR BUST!

BRIEF OVERVIEW

Nothing can be accomplished successfully in life without either trust in your-self or in others. No good relationships-whether family or friends-can be formed without trust. This lesson will show younger children why trust is so important.

MATERIALS NEEDED

• 4 balloons (any colors)

TIME NEEDED

15-20minutes

OBJECTIVE

Students will be able to relate their internal feelings about trust to their own actions and how these actions make others see trust in them.

PROCEDURES

The leader should hold a balloon. Then, a student volunteer will be asked to come to the front of the room. The child will be given a long straight pin. Tell the class to listen to some sentences. If the sentence makes them feel pleas-ant, raise their hand (and the leader should say, "This is a trustful action"). If it makes them feel unpleasant, keep their hands in their laps (and have the child with the pin pop the balloon). Do this using the following sentences:

• My teacher keeps his/her promises to our class. (This is a trustful action)
• I always tell the truth. (This is a trustful action)
• My best friend told me that I was the best at jump rope, but then she went to another girl and told her that she was better than me! (pops balloon)
• A boy pushed me out of the lunch line when I was looking away from him. (pops balloon)
• My friend promised to bring me a piece of candy today and she did! (This is a trustful action)
• I did all my chores today without being reminded. (This is a trustful action)
• I know I cannot believe a word she tells me! (pops balloon)

• My mom asked my sister to take me to school this morning, but as soon as we got away from mom, my sister said she was in a hurry and left me. (pops balloon)

Now, the leader should ask the class to talk about the meaning of trust-BELIEVING THAT WHAT IS SAID OR PROMISED WILL BE DONE. Have the students talk about their feelings when someone does not do what he/she promised.

Think of words that have the same meaning as TRUST (the leader should write these on the board for grades PreK-1). Grades 2-3 can use the worksheet on the next page to complete the acrostic.

FOLLOW-UP QUESTIONS

1. Do you want to be a person that is trusted by others? Why?

2. Do you want to choose friends that you can trust? Explain.

3. If someone accidentally makes a mistake, should you never trust them again? (Of course not.) What can you do to decide if it was just a mistake. (Talk it over with that person.)

4. When you aren't sure whether to trust a person after they have made you feel bad or uncomfortable, what should you do? (Talk it over with an adult you can trust.)

OPTIONAL ENDINGS

PreK-1: For the remainder of today and tomorrow, praise students that have done something trustworthy (i.e. finished the classwork, brought in signed papers, etc.) and put their name on a big balloon drawn on the chalkboard. Send home a "TRUST" report card to those students.

2-3: In student journals, have children write about "I want to be trusted because..."

Activity 21:
TRUST/LOVE CONNECTION

BRIEF OVERVIEW

Connecting the concept of trust is sometimes difficult for children-especially those children who have experienced either emotionally or physically abusive situations. Therefore, through the use of a read aloud story of a stray dog, children can be led to understand that trust has to be both "learned and earned". The fact that we can trust some people, but not every person will be discussed.

MATERIALS NEEDED

- *A Dog of My Own* by Jack Canfield and Mark Vicor Hansen from the *Chicken Soup for Little Souls* series.
- "Trust" Worksheet

TIME NEEDED

15 minutes

OBJECTIVES

The students will be able to define the meaning of trust. The students will identify the trusting characters in the book.

PROCEDURES

Have the children sit on a "Reading Rug" or somewhere in the room that they can be comfortable while they listen to the leader read aloud *A Dog of My Own*.

FOLLOW-UP QUESTIONS

1. What had mom promised Ben at the beginning of the story?

2. Did Ben get the pet he thought he would? Why or why not?

3. Did the dog trust Kelly and Ben when they went to get him? What feelings did the dog show at first? (Fear, etc.)

4. When did the dog begin to trust people around him more-especially Ben and Kelly?

5. Were Ben and Kelly able to get the dog to trust them the first day? How long did it take them?
   **The leader should re-read the last page of the book. Then ask the children if they can understand that sometimes TRUSTING someone takes a little or a lot of time. We must earn trust-just like Ben did with his dog. That's why we must be kind and keep our promises.

6. Tell me why TRUST is so important to you.

OPTIONAL ENDINGS

K-2: Using the attached worksheet, allow students to color the letters spelling "TRUST" and draw a picture describing the story they just heard about trust.

3-5: Have students work cooperatively to form a bulletin board with the "Trust" acrostic and their original thoughts on trust written by each letter.

Activity 21: Trust Worksheet

_____

_____

_____

_____

_____

Character Under Construction

COVER WITH A ROOF OF RESPECT!

🔑 Keys to RESPECT

🔑 Respect yourself.

🔑 Think of one good thing that others respect about you.

🔑 Respect others by being courteous and kind.

🔑 Respect cannot be bought.

🔑 Respect must be earned.

🔑 If we respect authority (or laws), we are much safer.

🔑 Respect the property of others.

🔑 Respect your body.

🔑 Respect your physical health by eating properly and exercising regularly.

🔑 Respect your emotional health by allowing yourself some quiet time each day.

🔑 When showing respect for others (parents, teachers, friends, etc.), you are setting a good example for those watching you.

🔑 R - E - S - P - E - C - T = Respect for Excellence Shows Peoples Exceptional Character Traits!

🔑 Learn to respect yourself and others by practicing respect daily.

🔑 Respect your teachers.

Cover With A Roof Of Respect!

(Sample Parent Letter)

Dear Parent(s)/Guardian(s):

RESPECT is a topic younger children need to be taught. Our Character Education lessons will focus on RESPECT for ourselves, others, and property. Expect to see some of our work coming home.

If you could obtain a copy of *The Rainbow Fish* either through the library or a book store, this would be a wonderful tool to read to your child about self-respect.

One topic that is suggested for you to discuss with your child is respecting his or her own body. This is relative to our health lessons which pertain to healthy foods, no drugs, etc. The relationship to respect is important here for your child.

Thanks for your continued support of our Good Character studies!

Sincerely,

Activity 22:
RAKING IN RESPECT

BRIEF OVERVIEW

This lesson enhances awareness of actions each of us can take so that others will respect us more! Words can be added to coordinate this with a special vocabulary lesson!

MATERIALS NEEDED

- *The Random house Book of Poetry for Children* (or other children's Literature selection on "Self-Respect" Found in the school library)
- "RAKING UP RESPECT" worksheet
- Crayons
- Scissors
- Glue

TIME NEEDED

20 minutes

OBJECTIVES

The students will learn the meaning of respect and become aware of the relationship of self-respect and good character habits.

PROCEDURES

Ask students to share something each student likes about himself/herself. The leader should write the good character traits on one side of the board (such as "..kind..","..nice..",...thoughtful..",etc. Now, write on the other side of the board some opposites (such as "..mean..", "..hurtful..", "..disobey..", etc.). A class discussion can follow in which students share the type of person each wants to become.

Now, read aloud one of the following from The Random House Book of Poetry for Children: "*What Is Pink*" by Christina Rosetti, "*Me I AM!*" by Jack Prelutsky, "*Just Me!*" by Margaret Hillert or a selection of the leader's choice on "Self-Respect". These selections can lead children to understand the concept of self-respect more.

Finally, begin to question students about how they gain respect from others around them such as: friends, parents, and teachers. After they have chosen ways, give them the "RAKING UP RESPECT" worksheet with safety scissors and glue. Have them cut out the rake prongs that have the words related to self-respect and glue on to the rake head.

FOLLOW-UP QUESTIONS

1. What is something you plan to do better so you will respect yourself more?

2. If you respect yourself, does that help you become a happier person? Explain and tell why.

3. When you are nice to someone who has had a bad day, how can that improve your self-respect?

OPTIONAL ENDINGS

K-2: Have each child agree to take the "RAKE" worksheet to either a parent, grandparent, aunt, or uncle and explain "self-respect" (if not able to do this, have the child explain to the leader at a convenient time).

3-5: Make a class art chart (or sentence strips) with room for each student to write with a colored marker a sentence about self-respect (they could use one or more words on the rake prongs). Have the child put his/her name by the sentence he/she wrote and display the sentences in the hallway or classroom!

Activity 22: Raking Up Respect

(cut out and attach these rake prongs to the rake head on page 95)

KIND

MEAN

NICE

HARD WORKING

HONEST

LIAR

LAZY

RESPONSIBLE

TAKE TURNS

PUSH

YELL

FOLLOW RULES

Activity 22:
Raking Up Respect

Activity 23:
"SEEK AND RESPECT" PROPERTY POWER!

BRIEF OVERVIEW

One commonly overlooked practice of character is respecting the property of other people and public places. Many times children simply do not think about such small individual acts such as littering, knocking something over, stepping on something that has fallen on the floor, etc. (This is most effective when following the lesson on self-respect titled "Raking in Respect" on page 92.)

MATERIALS NEEDED

• "Magnifying Glass Hat" worksheet

TIME NEEDED

15-20 minutes*

* 15 minutes first thing in the morning. 20 minutes at the end of the school day.

OBJECTIVE

Each student will identify various pieces of property that need to be taken care of (both individual and school properties).

PROCEDURES

Remind students of the meaning of respect. Tell them that today the class is going on a "Seek and Respect Hunt". The students will look for things within the school that need to be taken care of such as pencils, books, desks, etc. Reserve a place on the board (or chart paper) to list the property the children find. Several times (at least 3) during the day, ask the students to share any new property that needs to be "respected" or "cared for" and the leader should write it on the board.

After this game is understood, allow the students to make the "Magnifying Glass Hat" found on page 98. This will be worn by class members as they participate in the "Seek and Respect Hunt" throughout the school day.

At the end of the day, review all properties listed. Questions to be asked and discussed with the children are:

1. What will happen if you do not take care of your own property?
2. What will happen if you do not take care of the property of your friends?
3. Why should you be responsible for our school's property?
4. Who has the POWER to RESPECT the property of others?
5. Why is RESPECT so important to have as a good character trait?

FOLLOW-UP QUESTIONS

1. Ask the children to notice properties within their homes that need to be respected. Be prepared to discuss these at the first part of the following morning.

2. Have students name other places where property needs to be respected (i.e. all kinds of stores, public buildings, the homes of other people, etc.).

OPTIONAL ENDINGS

Have students adopt on area around their school yard that they will take care of.

K-2: Have old magazines, etc. available for students to cut out pictures of property that needs to be respected. Put these pictures on the bulletin board or a collage with PROPERTY POWER! at the top.

3-5: Ask the children to continue this "hunt" at home and bring back a list of properties at home that need to be respected!

Activity 23: "MAGNIFYING GLASS HAT" Pattern

(To be used with the "SEEK AND RESPECT" lesson.)

Activity 24:
ROVING RESPECT!

BRIEF OVERVIEW

Everywhere we go there is a constant need for respecting other people. Sometimes children think of respect as only a certain group - such as parents, teachers, etc. This lesson will help them realize that EVERYONE needs to be respected and valued as human beings!

MATERIALS NEEDED

- "Wheel of R-E-S-P-E-C-T worksheet
- Crayons
- Scissors

TIME NEEDED

15-20minutes

OBJECTIVES

The students will learn how respect is necessary with ALL people. The students will be able to describe ways to respect ALL people.

PROCEDURES

Hand out the "Wheel of R-E-S-P-E-C-T" worksheet found on page 101 to each student. The definition of respect will be reviewed. Talk about ways we should respect others. For example, we should be courteous, kind, show our good character to others, etc.

Next, discuss each "spoke" of the wheel on the worksheet. Talk about ways to RESPECT.

R - RIGHTS OF OTHERS
E - ELDERLY PEOPLE
S - SPECIAL NEEDS OF CERTAIN PEOPLE (physically challenged, etc.)
P - PARENTS
E - EVERYONE!
C - CONCERNS OR FEARS OF OTHERS
T - TEACHERS

Allow children to color each spoke of the wheel a different color and cut the wheels out to be displayed. If the children are able to write a sentence about each statement, allow them extra time to do so.

FOLLOW-UP QUESTIONS

1. When do you see the least respect for people? Why do you think that happens?

2. When is it the hardest for you to respect other people? Why?

OPTIONAL ENDINGS

K-2: Design a large "Wheel of R-E-S-P-E-C-T" for display and write some of the children's comments during the class discussion on each "spoke" of the wheel.

3-5: Design a large "Wheel of R-E-S-P-E-C-T" and have students take turns writing their own statement of respect on one spoke with their names beside their statements.

Activity 24: WHEEL OF R-E-S-P-E-C-T

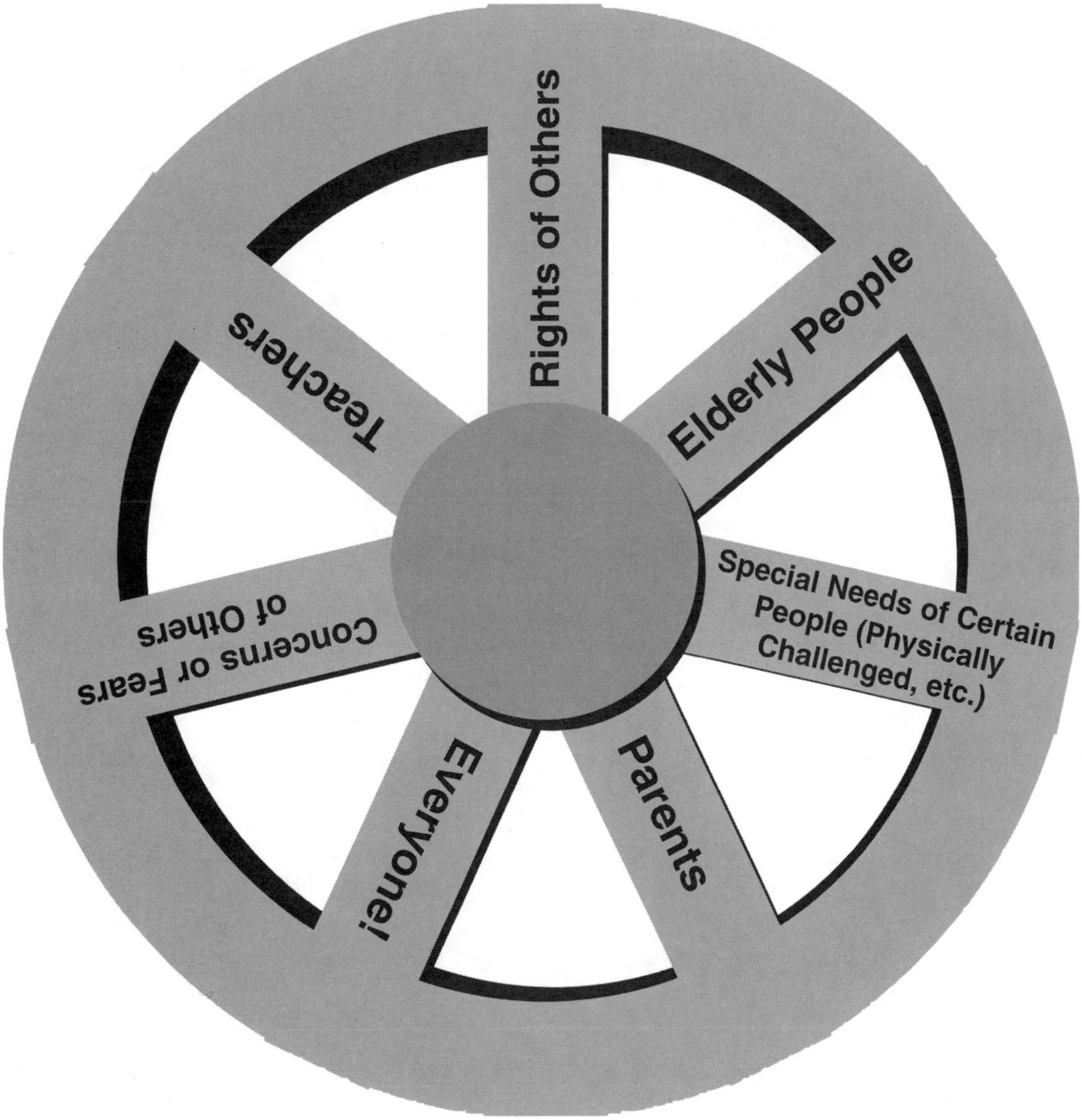

Rights of Others

Elderly People

Teachers

Special Needs of Certain People (Physically Challenged, etc.)

Concerns or Fears of Others

Parents

Everyone!

Character Under Construction

CEMENTING YOUR COURAGE!

🔑 Keys to COURAGE

🔑 It takes courage to ask for help.

🔑 Using your good character even when your friends make wrong choices takes real courage.

🔑 Remember to go to an adult you can trust (parent, teacher, counselor, principal, etc.) if you have any fears.

🔑 Learn to admit when you are wrong. That takes real courage!

🔑 When setting goals for yourself, realize courage will be needed all along the way as you accomplish those goals.

🔑 Realizing your potential and doing your very best in every task takes true courage.

🔑 Courage is when you stand up for what you know is right.

🔑 It takes courage to accept those things you cannot change and still continue to do the best you can with what you have now.

🔑 It takes courage to encourage others.

🔑 Courage is needed to set goals for yourself and to follow through with determination until your goals are reached.

🔑 Courage must be practiced and experienced.

🔑 Courage is when you keep the facts in your mind - not gossip or rumors.

🔑 It takes courage to accept the things we have no control over.

🔑 It takes courage to be kind to those who are unkind to you.

🔑 A loud voice is not a courageous voice.

🔑 It takes courage to smile when you don't really feel like it!

Cementing Your Courage!

(Sample Parent Letter)

Dear Parent(s)/Guardian(s):

As we all know, our children today - at a very young age - feel and experience peer pressure from friends and others they are in contact with each day. It has become a very real and important part of their learning experiences to understand the importance of practicing individual COURAGE when standing up to and facing such peer pressure.

The Character Education lessons we are covering in our classroom are designed to help children understand and be aware of courageous actions by both themselves and others around them. A discussion of certain fears will include ways to overcome those fears. I encourage you to discuss with your child some fear you had to overcome as a child (such as your first day at a new school, going to sleep in a dark room, etc.).

Let me know if your child has some unusual fear that could be discussed without using his or her name. Sometimes when children realize they aren't the only ones afraid, it makes the fear easier to overcome!

Thanks!

Sincerely,

Activity 25:
CEMENT COURAGE RECIPE

BRIEF OVERVIEW

Interaction and a "hands-on lab" will offer kinesthetic, visual, and auditory learners the opportunity to touch, see, and hear about courage at school. Individuals will have the opportunity to think about courageous acts already accomplished in order to prepare to be more courageous, when necessary, in the future.

MATERIALS NEEDED

- 3 cups dry cement
- 3 cups sand
- Disposable pan
- Water
- 24" stick or large disposable spoon (to combine mixture)
- Cement Mixer Worksheet
- **OPTIONAL: A toy cement mixer (to display and discuss)

TIME NEEDED

25-30 minutes*

OBJECTIVES

Individual students will form personal strategies for practicing positive courage. Class members will understand and be aware of courageous actions by self and peers.

PROCEDURES

The leader should define courage using a dictionary. A discussion with the class will follow which will talk about how class members are more courageous today than they were several years ago. For example, it took courage for each child to learn to crawl or walk or go to new places (such as school). The leader should then explain that courage is similar to cement and display the following recipe for making cement:

3 cups dry cement   3 cups sand   water to mix

Then, demonstrate to the class how cement is made. Once the mixture is poured into the pan, the leader should explain that "...once this cement hardens, it can only be broken by a large tool, such as a hammer or very, very cold or hot weather if it is left outside for a long time.

Explain that courage is similar to this cement. We have to mix our own <u>good character</u> with <u>strong will power to make the right choices and decide it is OK to be different if we disagree with those around us</u>. Once we have the courage to stand up for what is right, then our courage will be hard to break (just like the cement).

Follow-up with a discussion of times courage is needed at school. For example, on a playground when a bully tries to pick a fight (it's more courageous and wise to walk away), or in the hall when everyone is pushing and shoving in line (and you choose not to be involved), etc.

FOLLOW-UP QUESTIONS

1. Are all of us afraid sometimes? How can we be more courageous and less afraid?

2. If you do show courage one day, but the next day it's "broken" a little, can you "re-build" your courage? How?

3. <u>Who</u> can break your courage (ie others, yourself, etc.)? How?

OPTIONAL ENDINGS

K-2: With the "Cement Mixer" worksheet, have the students tell the teacher how they can show courage at school and the teacher will write the statement below the picture (they can color the picture).

3-5: Let each student take the stick or mixing spoon and place a small "dent" in the cement mixture. Then remind them that even when their courage is "dented" or is weak one day, it is not completely gone. The rest of the mold is still solid.

ALL LEVELS: Have the class come up with <u>an original recipe for courage!</u>

Activity 25: Cement Mixer Worksheet

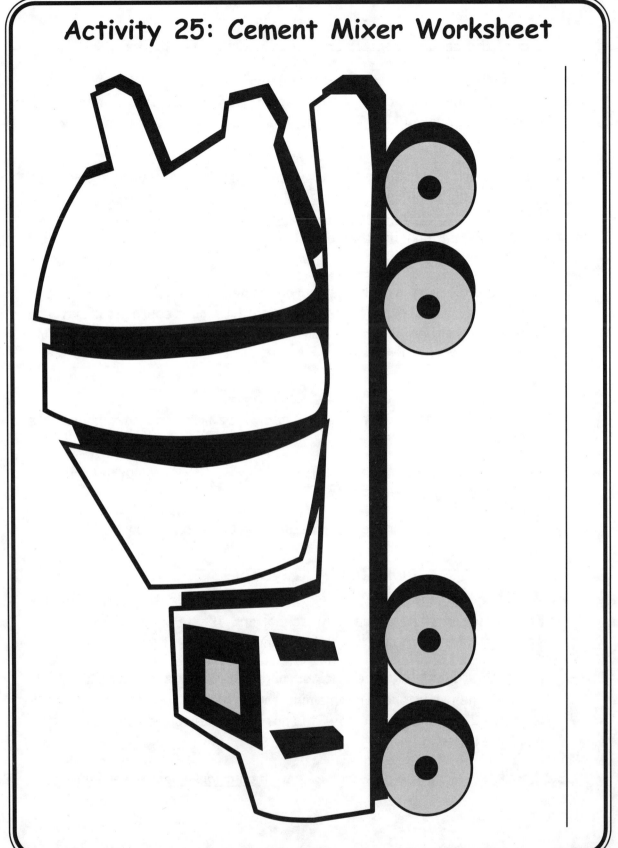

Activity 26:
COURAGE UNDER PRESSURE!

BRIEF OVERVIEW

Students will recognize and be more pro-active (not re-active) in situations which press them to follow the crowd. This lesson will help younger students prepare for peer pressure that is a result of interactions with other children in various places. Puppets and/or role play can be used to act out certain situations.

MATERIALS NEEDED

- "Courageous" Role Plays Worksheet
- 3 puppets (either 3 animals or 3 people-**do not mix**)
- * The help of an older student and/or a student in class is needed for the the 3rd puppet.
- **OPTIONAL: A "puppet stage" made of cardboard, if available.

TIME NEEDED

30minutes

OBJECTIVES

Students will learn the meanings of courage and pressure. Students will be able to formulate their own (or copy ideas presented in the lesson) coping mechanisms to handle courage under pressure.

PROCEDURES

(*NOTE: If puppets are not available, the same effect of this lesson can be obtained by having students to role play.)

Introduce the puppets (by name) to the class. Puppet #1 is "COURAGEOUS CATHY or CODY", Puppet #2 is "LEADING LYDIA or LANTZ", and Puppet #3 is "FOLLOWING FELISSA or FREDDIE" (These names depend on the gender of your puppets!)

Next the leader should explain that Puppet #1 has to make some hard or courageous decisions when put under pressure by Puppets #2 and #3. Discuss with the class the meanings of courageous and pressure (especially peer pressure). Use the play on page 111 to enact three situations that require courage. Follow each situation with a class discussion so that students can work through similar areas in their own lives that may require them to have a plan to act with courage!

FOLLOW-UP QUESTIONS

1. When you were small what were some times you were afraid and how did you get over those feelings?

2. Where are some places you need to show courage?

3. Who are some of the people you can depend on to help you when courage is needed?

OPTIONAL ENDINGS

K-2: Have some older students come to the classroom to present a role play and/or talk about courageous acts.

3-5: Ask each student to interview one adult for a project using the following QUESTIONS:

1) Have you ever been afraid?
2) When and of what were you afraid?
3) How did you handle this fear?
4) Who is the most courageous person you have ever known? Why?

*Bring these answers back to class to discuss. This is a great LANGUAGE ARTS assignment and includes basic interviewing skills!

Activity 27:
COURAGEOUS Role Plays

(For use with Puppets and/or Role Plays)

Setting:

Puppet 2: Hey, Felissa (or Freddie), when Alonzo gets on the bus at the next stop let's take his book bag and pour everything out of it all over the bus!

Puppet 3: Yeah! He's just a little kid and he can't do anything about it.

Puppet 1: Act as if she/he is thinking to himself/herself. What can I do to help Alonzo? He's new on the bus and he won't have anyone to take up for him. But, if I take up for him, my friends will get mad at me and they might play a trick on me next time! I won't feel good inside if I don't help out, but I'm scared! What can I do?

…Allow time for the class to offer suggestions and then have the puppets act out a couple solutions…

Setting:

Puppet 2: NO, you cannot play frisbee® with us. Now, go away or you'll be sorry. You aren't in our club. (4th puppet/person hangs his head and begins to leave.)

Puppet 3: (Laughing) Guess you told him! You are real cool!

Puppet 1: Well I don't feel cool. It's really mean to hurt someone's feelings. Why can't he play with us?
…How is Puppet 1 acting with courage?…What if his friends stop playing with him?…What would you do if this happened on your playground?…

Setting is in the hall rest room...

Puppet 2: (Laughing and pointing to the wall.) Look what I wrote with marker on this wall! I bet nothing will get this off! And-no one will ever know who did it except for the three of us!

Puppet 3: Wow! You've got nerve. That's against school rules and everything.

Puppet 2: Well, let's all write on this wall to prove we're best friends. We're the tough kids!

Puppet 3: OK-keep a watch out for others and give me the marker (he/she pretends to write on the wall).

Puppet 1: We can get in serious trouble for this!

Puppets 3 and 2 (together): CHICKEN..SCAREDY CAT!

...Have students suggest how they would react to this. The leader should write these ideas on the board or a piece of chart paper...Then discuss how following school rules can sometimes take courage!...

Activity 28:
CREATIVE COURAGE

BRIEF OVERVIEW

Children need practice and encouragement when performing in front of class-mates. For the more outgoing personalities, this may include teaching restraint from "over acting". For the shy children this may include praise and positive reinforcements. For any student, it takes courage when beginning to perform such things as reading, answering questions, reciting poetry, etc. in front of groups of peers. This lesson is designed to show creative ways to use courage to overcome such fears!

MATERIALS NEEDED

- *THERE'S A MONSTER UNDER MY BED!* (Children's book)
- *THE KISSING HAND* (Children's book)
- *In advance, send home and collect the Parent Questionnaire (on page 115)*

TIME NEEDED

10-30 minutes*

* Depending on the strategy to be used.

OBJECTIVE

Each student will be able to perform one task alone while other classmates observe.

PROCEDURES

The leader should need to do some preliminary "investigating" in the planning stages of this lesson. Prior to the actual lesson, find out what each child enjoys (a hobby, etc.). This information could be obtained by a short questionnaire to parents and/or conversations with the children. A sample questionnaire to be sent home can be found on page 115.

Without using names discuss certain fears that are normal for children such as fear of the dark, fear of new places, fear of crowds, etc. Read to the class *THERE'S A MONSTER UNDER MY BED!* And discuss the fear that was overcome. Also, *THE KISSING HAND* could be read and discussed to overcome the fear of separation from a parent(s).

FOLLOW-UP QUESTIONS

1. If you will, share with the class one way these stories and our discussion have helped you with one of your fears.

2. When you are afraid, what is one way you can become less afraid? (For example, talk about it with an adult.)

3. Have you ever overcome one of your fears? If so, what was it and how did you get over that fear?

OPTIONAL ENDINGS

Pre-K-1: Have them draw a picture of something they are afraid of and write on that picture what it is. Then, either send this home or discuss the fear individually with the child.

2-3: Ask the child to write (for extra credit) a story about their greatest fear and how they think they can get enough courage to overcome that fear.

Cementing Your Courage!

(Sample Parent Questionnaire)

Dear Parent(s)/Guardian(s):

Please take 3-5 minutes to fill in the blanks below and have your chid return this to me.

We are planning a lesson called "Creative Courage" in order for your child to be better prepared to read, talk, perform, etc. in front of his/her classmates!

Thanks for your help!

Parent QUESTIONS

_____

Child's Name

Favorite Games/Activities:

1)_____

2)_____

3)_____

Greatest Fears (if any)

_____

_____

** Please RETURN BY _____

Thanks!

BALANCE BEAMS OF EQUALITY/ FRIENDSHIP

Keys to EQUALITY

 All hearts are the same color.

 Person + Person = Persons (in any combination)

 When everyone works together, the task is completed faster and everyone is happier.

 ALL have worth and potential.

 Different eyes, hair, skin and personalities make the world a more diverse and attractive place!

 Self-control can be practiced and learned by ALL, if we just keep trying!

 Even when our circumstances seem unfair, we are all equal in the good we can give to the world.

Smiles bring positive results!

Balance Beams Of Equality/Friendship

(Sample Parent Letter)

Dear Parent(s)/Guardian(s):

Children go through phases of various feelings - some over-confident, some not so confident, and some balanced feelings of "I didn't do it the first time, but maybe I can the next time".

Part of growing is learning that each person has his or her talents, but not everyone is good at everything. We can help our children learn about friendships and equality by teaching lessons such as these. Not only will each child feel better about his or herself, each child will recognize and be more positive about others - no matter who the "other" is or what the "other" is able to do.

Thanks for your continued support with our Character Education series of lessons!

Sincerely,

Activity 29:
LESS THAN, GREATER THAN, OR EQUAL TO?

BRIEF OVERVIEW

This lesson is great to combine with math lessons. In K-2 this lesson could include teaching in different shapes. In 3-5 this lesson could be taught with equalities/inequalities of numbers. The focus is to show students that while we are equal in value as people, we have different talents to contribute to the world!

MATERIALS NEEDED

- •
- • Glue
- • "Unequal Shapes" worksheet colored paper (one sheet per student)

TIME NEEDED

30 minutes

OBJECTIVES

The students will learn that different pieces can work together to form a whole. The students will be able to discuss some ways each of them are different, yet each of them is important to the class as a whole.

PROCEDURES

Introduce the lesson by explaining that different parts work together to form a whole. For example, a bicycle has wheels and handlebars. They look different, but can you ride the bike if you take the wheels off? Or can you ride the bike without the handlebars? But, when these parts work together, what happens?

Ask the students about their class. Can we have a class without the teacher? Is the teacher the same size and shape of each of you? Do all of you look exactly alike? Then, even if we are not equal in size, shape, or appearance, are we all still important? Even if we are all different, can we still work together in this classroom to learn important things?

© 2000 YouthLight, Inc.

Next, give each student a pair of safety scissors, glue, an "Unequal Shapes" worksheet, and one sheet of colored paper. Instruct the students to cut out shapes and try to make a picture using these shapes, using the color sheet as a background. After a few minutes, show the class on the board how to make a train!

FOLLOW-UP QUESTIONS

1. Did the shapes work together to form something special?

2. How is our class like these shapes? Can we work together each day to be a special class?

3. How can we all work together equally to be important members of this class?

OPTIONAL ENDINGS

K-2: The leader could write on large chart paper comments made by class members of how each of them can contribute or help the class become better. This could be displayed with train pictures around it!

3-5: Students (either individually or in small groups) could construct various objects from a variety of shapes. These original designs could be covers for essays "Working Together We Can Do Bigger Things!"

Activity 29: Unequal Shapes Worksheet

Activity 30:
THE SEE-SAW GAME!

BRIEF OVERVIEW

This game sparks the creativity of the students to express their views of equality and friendship traits. The goal of the class is to be considered "winners" by having the balance tray "in balance" at the end of the questions!

MATERIALS NEEDED

- Balance tray with 26 equal weights (from science lab or cafeteria)

TIME NEEDED

15 minutes

OBJECTIVE

Children will be able to recognize and put into action more fairness to all students.

PROCEDURES

Lead the class in a discussion about fairness, equality, and friendship. The balance tray with weights will be placed at the front of the classroom. Explain that you are going to read 16 statements about friendships, equality, and/or fairness. One class member will be called on to respond to each statement. The RIGHT side of the balance tray is the FAIR or EQUAL side. The LEFT side of the balance tray is the UNFAIR or UNEQUAL side.

Statements are to be read by leader and responded to by students individually. FAIR is for RIGHT side of balance tray and UNFAIR is for LEFT side of balance tray.

1. Johnny gets to eat candy during class and the remainder of the class does not. UNFAIR
2. Omar must leave class to take his medicine while the remainder of the class continues to work. FAIR
3. Betsy gets to be the class leader 3 days in a row. The other class members take turns being the leader each day. UNFAIR

4. Heidi is tall and Mandy is short. FAIR (We are all different and special!)
5. Missy, Mary, Shondell, and Dan are starting a "good character club" at recess. Anyone can join that uses good character traits such as telling the truth and showing respect. FAIR
6. Jack likes being a bully and pushing others around. UNFAIR
7. Again, Jack likes being a bully and pushing others around. However, this time he is disciplined. FAIR
8. Timmy has a broken leg. He gets to ride in a wheel chair for several weeks, but others still have to walk. FAIR (Timmy's situation is something he really cannot help.)
9. Missy gets to use the slide every day at recess and always go first. The other children take turns. UNFAIR
10. Marley has short hair and Cyndal has long hair. FAIR
11. Angela's parents are from Germany, Marlene's parents are from Washington state, and Meg's parents are from South Carolina. FAIR
12. The leader lets 14 people go to the library whenever they want to, but not the other 6 people in the class. They can only go on Tuesdays. UNFAIR
13. Jared shares toys at recess with his best friends, but he does not share toys with others. UNFAIR
14. Marshall or Eddie run errands for the leader every day. Marshall and Eddie get to raise the flag every day. They seem to get to do everything! UNFAIR
15. Mary, Kisha, Michael, and Terry all try to do their best in Math, but it's very hard. Hal's grandmother volunteers to help them 30 minutes each day so they can understand the math better. FAIR
16. Cal agrees to be Hank's friend, but not Jason's. UNFAIR

Now, the class discussion will center around how some things are fair because of SITUATIONS and not because of people (and the opposite applies as well).

FOLLOW-UP QUESTIONS

1. Are you always fair? Think of one time recently that you were fair. Share this with the class.
2. How can you be more fair this week? Share this with the class.

OPTIONAL ENDINGS

All grade levels - Use the book *FREAK THE MIGHTY*, by R. Philbrick to foster further discussion of friendship, equality, and loyalty.

Activity 31:
Friends

BRIEF OVERVIEW

This activity and the poem that follows will help students to realize that by practicing the good character traits in this book, new friends can be made and old friends can remain.

MATERIALS NEEDED

 • Poem "Friends" on page 127
(reproduce one for each student)

TIME NEEDED

30 minutes

OBJECTIVES

Children will discuss and recognize the character traits necessary to make and keep friends at school. Children will also be able to visualize how the school can be a better place by using these traits daily.

PROCEDURES

Read the poem "Friends" and discuss the good character traits in upper case lettering. Allow students to review the meanings of each of these traits. The leader will then point out the "opposites" in the poem (i.e. short/high, weak/strong, etc.). These show areas where we are not all equal. Then the leader will ask:

- Are all your friends the same or equal?
- Are YOU the same or equal to everyone else?
- Is everyone a good reader, a good athlete, a good singer, etc.?
- Does that mean we cannot be friends?
- How can being different HELP your friendship with another person?

After this discussion, have each student draw a scene showing him/herself with at least three other friends. Then have each student write a sentence or paragraph describing how he/she is different (a positive difference) from the other three friends in the picture.

FOLLOW-UP QUESTIONS

1. After completing this lesson are you glad we are all different? Why

2. Even though we are different and are friends, how are we alike? (i.e. feelings, etc.)

3. How do the other good character traits we have studied help you make new friends and keep your old friends?

OPTIONAL ENDINGS

K-2: Display pictures of children in the class at recess and/or lunch. Include all members of the class in various pictures. Have the children tell about their "class family" and how all are different but equal. Put these thoughts down on large chart paper for a really cute bulletin board!

3-5: Have students work individually (for a project) or in groups (for a Language Arts activitiy) to compose 2-4 more standzas for the "Friends" poem.

Friends

I come to school every day,
To work and work, and yes—to play!
Now it's OK to play alone,
But I can do that when I'm at home!

In school new friends I like to meet
And I can do that if I'm sweet!
If I'm KIND and with a smile
I can make new friends all the while!

Some friends are short and some are tall,
Some jump up high and some may fall,
Some have short hair and some have long,
And some are weak and some are strong!

With COURAGE, RESPECT, and TRUST,
And of course, HONESTY is a must,
Then good MANNERS I can show,
And my ATTITUDE will really glow!

No— we aren't all equal in every way,
But we still can have fun every day.
It takes good character to enjoy,
Each and every girl and boy!

Character Under Construction

A SHOVEL FULL OF SHARING & COOPERATION!

🔑 Keys to SHARING/COOPERATION

🔑 Share your friends.

🔑 Be a good listener.

🔑 Concentrate on what others tell you by looking at the person as he or she speaks to you.

🔑 Enjoy sharing!

🔑 Sharing is to cooperation as caring is to kindness.

🔑 To cooperate is to work and grow together.

🔑 Share and you'll always receive something in return.

🔑 S - H - A - R - E = Share Happiness And Real Experiences.

🔑 When sharing ideas with another person and you both decide to keep one idea each - you have successfully made a compromise.

🔑 We must learn to share first and next we must learn to cooperate.

🔑 Cooperation is a character trait we must possess.

🔑 Team cooperation makes any job easier for each team member.

🔑 When the band plays a song, each instrument must help out, just as each of us must cooperate (or work together) with each other.

© 2000 YouthLight, Inc.

A Shovel Full Of Sharing & Cooperation!

(Sample Parent Letter)

Dear Parent(s)/Guardian(s):

Prior to beginning school, you have worked very hard to teach your child the concept of sharing with others. Once in school, children realize there are so MANY MORE people to share with on a daily basis. For some this is easier than others. As children progress, teachers consistently offer opportunities for cooperation among class members which advances the idea of sharing even more!

As we continue to stress good character traits in our class, please be aware that we are currently working on traits of SHARING and COOPERATION. Please talk with your child about our lessons and class discussions. As you follow through at home with these thoughts, it may even make a difference with brothers, sisters, and neighborhood friends for your child!

Thanks for your reinforcement of our Character Education lessons! You are helping your child for a lifetime!

My best,

Activity 32:
COOL COOPERATION GAME!

BRIEF OVERVIEW

This is a great "rainy day" game or a wonderful activity to teach the concept of cooperation to 2nd - 5th graders!

MATERIALS NEEDED

- Tokens
- Caller cards
- "Cooperation" activity sheet

TIME NEEDED

5-10 minutes per game

OBJECTIVE

The student will identify a variety of ways to cooperate in all areas of life (at school, home, in stores, etc.).

PROCEDURES

Each student will match a square on the "cooperation" sheet with the cards called out by the caller. Tokens are placed as the cards are called, the first player to get tokens horizontal, vertical, or diagonal calls out COOPERATION! The winner gets to be the caller for the next game, etc.

FOLLOW UP QUESTIONS

1. What are some ways you have to share or cooperate that were not mentioned on the cards?

2. Will you have to share or cooperate more or less as you get older? Why?

OPTIONAL ENDINGS

K-1 Have the younger classroom visit a 4th or 5th grade classroom during this game as it is being played and discussed. The younger children could place the tokens as the "4th or 5th grade mentors" tell them to do so. Then as the discussion about sharing and cooperation takes place, the little ones will not only learn but will be encouraged to follow the role modeling of the older classmates!

Activity 32: Caller Cards

Be Kind	Share Books	Respect Others	Good Attitude	Help Others
Good Manners	Listen	Work	Follow Rules	Be Dependable
Set a Goal	Cooperate	Finish Classwork	Water Flowers	Feed Dog
Do Homework	Take Out Trash	Respect Yourself	Make Your Bed	Tell the Truth
Study	Do Your Best	Wait Your Turn	Raise Your Hand	Share Toys
Sit Down In the Bus	Walk In the Halls	Obey School Rules	Brush Your Teeth	Get Your Papers Signed
Take Turns on the Playground Equipment	Treat Others Kind	Smile!	Congratulate Others	Pick Up Trash on the Floor

Activity 32: COOL COOPERATION GAME!

Be Kind	Follow Rules	Work
Share Books	FREE SPACE	Listen
Respect Others	Help Others	Good Manners

Be Dependable	Set a Goal	Do Your Homework
Cooperate	FREE SPACE	Pick Up Trash on the Floor
Finish Classwork	Water Flowers	Smile!

Activity 32: COOL COOPERATION GAME!

Tell the Truth	Cooperate	Make Your Bed
Congratulate Others	FREE SPACE	Respect Yourself
Sit Down In the Bus	Smile!	Water Flowers
Take Turns on the Playground Equipment	Good Manners	Walk in the Halls
Raise Your Hand	FREE SPACE	Take Out Trash
Finish Classwork	Treat Others Kind	Do Your Best

Activity 32: COOL COOPERATION GAME!

Follow Rules	Respect Others	Walk in the Halls
Listen	FREE SPACE	Finish Classwork
Smile!	Brush Your Teeth	Good Attitude

Treat Others Kind	Share Books	Cooperate
Take Turns on the Playground Equipment	FREE SPACE	Feed Dog
Raise Your Hand	Work	Be Dependable

Activity 32: COOL COOPERATION GAME!

Good Attitude	Share Toys	Get Your Papers Signed
Do Your Best	FREE SPACE	Study
Work	Help Others	Brush Your Teeth

Listen	Obey School Rules	Study
Share Books	FREE SPACE	Water Flowers
Do Homework	Walk In the Halls	Tell the Truth

Activity 32: COOL COOPERATION GAME!

Walk In the Halls	Be Dependable	Sit Down In the Bus
Smile!	FREE SPACE	Make Your Bed
Follow Rules	Study	Congratulate Others

Pick Up Trash on the Floor	Treat Others Kind	Respect Yourself
Listen	FREE SPACE	Water Flowers
Good Manners	Set a Goal	Take Out Trash

138

Activity 32: COOL COOPERATION GAME!

Study	Raise Your Hand	Good Manners
Wait Your Turn	FREE SPACE	Share Books
Walk In the Halls	Congratulate Others	Good Attitude

Raise Your Hand	Set a Goal	Help Others
Sit Down In the Bus	FREE SPACE	Good Manners
Smile!	Feed Dog	Respect Yourself

Activity 32: COOL COOPERATION GAME!

Do Your Best	Be Dependable	Finish Classwork
Get Your Papers Signed	FREE SPACE	Cooperate
Work	Follow Rules	Make Your Bed

Study	Good Attitude	Take Turns on the Playground Equipment
Pick Up Trash on the Floor	FREE SPACE	Follow Rules
Listen	Water Flowers	Be Kind

Activity 32: COOL COOPERATION GAME!

Raise Your Hand	Brush Your Teeth	Do Homework
Share Toys	FREE SPACE	Set a Goal
Walk In the Halls	Respect Others	Smile!

Treat Others Kind	Obey School Rules	Cooperate
Work	FREE SPACE	Good Manners
Tell the Truth	Respect Yourself	Feed Dog

Activity 32: COOL COOPERATION GAME!

Do Homework	Share Books	Study
Make Your Bed	FREE SPACE	Follow Rules
Take Turns on the Playground Equipment	Be Kind	Feed Dog

Take Out Trash	Cooperate	Get Your Papers Signed
Listen	FREE SPACE	Help Others
Wait Your Turn	Obey School Rules	Be Dependable

142

Activity 32: COOL COOPERATION GAME!

Feed Dog	Sit Down In the Bus	Cooperate
Do Your Best	FREE SPACE	Get Your Papers Signed
Raise Your Hand	Good Attitude	Congratulate Others
Wait Your Turn	Good Manners	Set a Goal
Cooperate	FREE SPACE	Tell the Truth
Respect Others	Brush Your Teeth	Do Homework

Activity 32: COOL COOPERATION GAME!

Set a goal	Do Homework	Follow Rules
Be Dependable	FREE SPACE	Study
Walk In the Halls	Good Attitude	Feed Dog

Cooperate	Do Homework	Help Others
Congratulate Others	FREE SPACE	Share Books
Sit Down In the Bus	Treat Others Kind	Water Flowers

Activity 33:
COOPERATION AT HOME!

BRIEF OVERVIEW

This lesson is a literature discussion of cooperation. Children will be encouraged to practice this lesson with parents and other family members.

MATERIALS NEEDED

- *A Chair for My Mother* by Vera Williams (K-2) OR *Across Five Aprils* by Irene Hunt (3-5) OR *Stories of Cooperation* by Henry Billings (any age)

TIME NEEDED

20 minutes

OBJECTIVE

Children will understand and be able to apply various views of cooperation through literature stories - ideally told by the leader (with much enthusiasm)!

PROCEDURES

The leader should read one of the selected stories and children will discuss the meaning of sharing/cooperation. Next the children will design their own "story" through pictures and one or two sentences about how they cooperate in similar ways. The leader can then display these for the cooperative bulletin board.

FOLLOW-UP QUESTIONS

1. Explain how this story will help me share and cooperate more in my home.
2. Who, in my home, do I need to share and cooperate more with today? Why?

OPTIONAL ENDINGS

K-2 Read and discuss *It's Mine* by C. Bonsall.

3-5 Read, discuss, and have the children write about *A Tale of Three Trees*.

REACHING YOUR CONSTRUCTION GOAL!

Keys to GOAL SETTING

 Decide to IMPROVE on ONE thing TODAY.

 To reach your goal you must persevere.

 The word QUIT must NEVER be in your vocabulary.

 Set daily goals . . . keep trying (persevere).

 Set monthly goals . . . and keep trying (persevere).

 Set yearly goals . . . and keep trying (persevere).

 Little goals accomplished = Bigger goals mastered.

 It takes climbing one step at a time to reach the top of the stairs.

 If you fall back one step, decide to climb forward two steps.

 Talk with someone you trust about your goals.

 We are sometimes like little puppies. We must run after the ball many times before we become good at bringing it back.

 Practice . . . practice . . . practice helps us be successful!

Reaching Your Construction Goal!

(Sample Parent Letter)

Dear Parent(s)/Guardian(s):

Children sometimes think only of today! While this can be healthy, children also need to become aware of how their actions today may affect tomorrow—and the rest of their lives!

Through our Character Education unit on "Goal Setting" our class will be learning how to use good character traits to set daily, weekly, and yearly goals for themselves. We will be using children's literature, autobiographies, and visuals to help children *see* the importance of setting personal goals.

Since as the parent(s), you are your child's greatest resource, please listen to and discuss with your child the goals he/she has in mind currently. Encourage, encourage, encourage...the communication! Also, praise, praise, praise...your child's successes as he/she accomplishes the short term goals!

Thanks for your continued support! Working together, we can help your child improve the future!

Sincerely,

Activity 34:
GAINING OUR GOALS!

BRIEF OVERVIEW

This lesson will help establish the meaning of short term goals - ones that can be reached within a few short weeks (or less). Individual goals will be defined, charted, and techniques to achieve these goals will be devised.

MATERIALS NEEDED

- A book on reaching goals (see resource list or school media center)
- One index card per student
- Tape

TIME NEEDED

30 minutes

OBJECTIVE

Students will set and attempt to accomplish at least one individual short term goal during the next week.

PROCEDURES

Explain to the class that short term goals are ones that each person is able to make for themselves and reach in a short period of time (for younger children this might be one day, for older elementary children this might be one week or month).

Read the book of your choice on goal setting (or perseverance) to the class. Discuss this book and the meaning of setting goals and staying with these goals until accomplished. Point out that sometimes we do not reach these goals without making some mistakes. The key is to keep on trying!

Now, have each student think of one thing they really want to accomplish quickly (such as make a better grade on a spelling test, better behavior in the class, listen more attentively, etc.). The leader should list (for the younger students) or the student will list ONE short term goal on an index card. This card will be taped to the student's desk. At the end of the day (or week) the leader and student will access if that goal has been reached —how and why.

Once this goal has been accomplished, allow the student to add to this goal (an extension). This might be a better grade in spelling and math next week, or better behavior in the lunchroom as well as the classroom, etc.).

FOLLOW-UP QUESTIONS
(to be done during the goal assessment time):

1. How did you feel when you reached your goal? Why?

2. Was is difficult - why or why not?

3. Did setting a goal help you improve yourself? How?

OPTIONAL ENDINGS

K-2: Make a goal setting wall and each time a child reaches his/her goal, put a star on the index card and place that child's card on the wall!

3-5: Allow the older students to go into the younger classrooms and share some of their short term goals and how it is important to keep trying to reach these goals. The older students might even devise a role play situation and present the drama to a younger class!

Activity 35:
CLIMBING YOUR STAIRS—REACHING YOUR GOALS!

BRIEF OVERVIEW

This lesson will focus on reaching long-term goals. With the example of a stair case (on the worksheet) students can visualize how short-term goals can lead to successfully reaching long-term goals. This lesson is excellent to tie in with the School-to-Work awareness idea prevalent with elementary age children!

MATERIALS NEEDED

- "Stairs" worksheet
* Optional - *Junebug* by A. Mead (a book on work, self-discipline, and goals)

TIME NEEDED

| 30 minutes |

PROCEDURES

The leader should write on the board the following statements under the Goal Setting heading:

LITTLE GOALS ACCOMPLISHED = BIGGER GOALS MASTERED
And
IT TAKES CLIMBING ONE STEP AT A TIME TO REACH THE TOP OF THE STAIRS.

Give each student a "Stair" worksheet. Take the short-term goal(s) accomplished and list on the bottom one, two, or three steps. Then set a goal for the TOP step. (For example, if the child has set goals to improve spelling and math, the long term goal could be to complete the current grade successfully by year end. Or, if the behavior in the class and lunchroom have improved, the long term goal could be to get a citizenship or good character award at the end of the year.)

These "Stairs" will be placed in a class notebook. Review with the individual children their progress periodically (ideally each week). When the long term goal is reached, the leader should make sure to present a certificate, etc. to that child to take home!

FOLLOW-UP QUESTIONS
(to be asked as the periodic reviews take place):

1. Do you feel you are on your way to reaching your long-term goal? Why or why not?

2. Is there a way to accomplish this goal faster? How?

3. What are you feeling or thinking as you try to take a new "step" toward your long-term goal?

4. Have you had any "steps" backward? If so, what did you do (or what can you do) to start moving up the "steps" again?

OPTIONAL ENDINGS

K-2: Set short term skill goals for academics on class charts. Allow students to view their progress toward a long-term goal. (The thing to be careful of here is to acknowledge EFFORT more than SKILL mastery since all children master skills at various paces!)

3-5: Work with the Physical Education, Music, and Art teachers to stress PRACTICE, PRACTICE, PRACTICE in reaching any goal. These teachers may want to work toward a joint project that will give children long term successes in various areas!

Activity 35: "STAIR" worksheet

Long Term Goals

Short Term Goals

Activity 36:
GOALS FOR LIFE!

BRIEF OVERVIEW

Most people dream. Children are no exception. They may have a dream of being a professional athlete, a computer whiz, a princess, or many other things. Some are realistic dreams and some may need to be refined as the children grow. We need to allow them to dream over the years, help them set realistic goals, and help them devise plans to accomplish their life goals. This lesson is to be done in coordination with Reading/Literature/Social Studies classes.

MATERIALS NEEDED

- Selected autobiographies of successful people in history (for example, Presidents of the United States, athletic figures, dancers, special parents, etc.)

TIME NEEDED

Several Class Periods

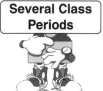

PROCEDURES

The teacher will lead the class in a study of the selected figures of history. Consistent and constant references will be made to life goals attained and how these people accomplished these goals.

Younger children will be asked to color pictures of these people or draw these people with a sentence about them. Next, the children will draw a picture of how they want to be seen when they "grow up".

Older children can be asked to identify some of the difficulties these historical figures encountered during the journey to reach their goals. Then these children can describe their goals, list the obstacles that need to be overcome (i.e. education, physical requirements, etc.), and discuss some alternate career possibilities for consideration, as well.

A "career fair" with several speakers (parents are ideal!) could be held so that various careers could be viewed in class. This could be done as a class or grade level!

FOLLOW-UP QUESTIONS

1. Did you learn about another career you might wish to set a long-term goal to achieve or did you stay with your first goal? Why and what did you learn?

2. What difficulties might you encounter in reaching your long-term goal?

3. How can you begin NOW to work toward this goal - at school and away from school?

OPTIONAL ENDINGS

Work with other teachers and classrooms to form a career wall in a central location with long term goals posted.

Use a school morning show or the announcements to interview people in various careers or talk about different careers and 3-4 sentences about what you need to prepare for that career.

Have a "dress-up" career day at the school.

DEPENDABLE BUILDERS!

🔑 Keys to DEPENDABILITY

🔑 Take the word CAN'T out of your vocabulary. Replace it with the word TRY.

🔑 Be enthusiastic and "up beat" about your duties.

🔑 When you make a mistake, simply admit it.

🔑 Decide to be dependable.

🔑 When you are dependable, you receive more freedom and responsibilities.

🔑 Being dependable means knowing you will do what you are asked when you are asked to complete it.

🔑 Being able to depend on yourself and your character, helps you build more confidence.

🔑 If you are a part of a team, you must be dependable, or the whole team will suffer.

🔑 Being a true friend requires dependability.

🔑 Dependability, trustworthiness and honesty are like links in a chain.

🔑 Find one dependable friend and you have the most valuable gift of your life.

🔑 You can receive so much encouragement from a dependable friend.

Dependable Builders!

(Sample Parent Letter)

Dear Parent(s)/Guardian(s):

Dependability is a character trait desired in people of all ages. You and I want our family, friends, co-workers, medical professionals, and all people we are in contact with to be dependable! We like to be able to *count on others to do what they say they are going to do.*

This is no different with our children. As children mature from toddlers, to young teenagers, we want to be able to depend on them to tell us the truth and be dependable in their chores and assignments, both at home and school. Finally, these teenagers become adults and the dependability that has become a part of their early lives is expected to be a segment of their adult motivation to get the job done—and well!

During the next few weeks, our class will be concentrating on the good character trait of dependability. Please listen and encourage your child in this area.

Thanks for your continued support and interest in the character of the children which are our future!

Sincerely

159

Activity 37:
DEPENDABILITY

BRIEF OVERVIEW   This lesson will introduce the meaning of dependability. Children will be encouraged to show their dependability at home and school as a major part of their good character actions.

MATERIALS NEEDED
- "I am Dependable" poem
* Optional - The teacher may read aloud from *The Book of Virtues* by William J. Bennett some of the stories concerning being trustworthy and dependable.

TIME NEEDED
15 minutes

PROCEDURE

Discuss as a class the meaning of dependable. How is the teacher dependable? How are you dependable as a student? How are your family members dependable? How are your friends dependable?

Encourage the class to learn the "I am Dependable" poem together and have them clap out the rhythm as they recite the words.

FOLLOW-UP QUESTIONS
(to be done the next morning):

1. After our lesson on being dependable, tell us how you were dependable when you left school yesterday afternoon?

2. How can you be dependable on the school bus or in the school halls?

3. How does being a dependable person help you?

OPTIONAL ENDINGS

K-2 Use the follow-up questions to write a class story on large chart paper about "Dependable Actions"

3-5 Give "Dependability" awards to children who "adopt" a younger child to read aloud to at least one time per week during the older child's recess!

I AM DEPENDABLE

I am dependable.
You can bet on me.
When I say I will help out
Success you plan to see!

I am dependable.
I mean just what I say!
The job I promise I will do
Will get done that very day!

I am dependable
At home and in my school.
There is no reason ever
To break any given rule.

I am dependable.
Why am I telling you?
Because I have good character
And SO CAN YOU!

Activity 38:
LINKS TO DEPENDABILITY

BRIEF OVERVIEW

This lesson is excellent to pull together the other character traits, such as honesty, responsibility, respect, goal setting, attitude, etc., and relate one to another. The visual of a paper chain (made by the children) is used.

MATERIALS NEEDED

- Discussion Cards
- Strips of construction paper (2" X 10") various colors
- Tape (or glue)
- Markers or Dark Pens

TIME NEEDED

25-35 minutes

OBJECTIVE

Each student will participate and identify dependable actions that are necessary to good character.

PROCEDURES

Use the following "discussion cards" to identify both dependable actions with at least one other good character action. Once these have been used and the relationships identified, ask each child to think of a good action they have done recently. (For younger children you can write these on strips of paper. The older children can write these themselves.)

After each child shares with the class their dependable action (and other) good character actions, the child will add to the chain his/her "link". A good idea is for the leader to model and begin the chain with his/her own action!

This can be repeated each day for several days until the good character "dependability chain" goes around the whole classroom!

FOLLOW-UP QUESTIONS

1. Do you think you could be dependable and still not have good character? Why or why not?

2. Why is dependability so important to our character?

3. When choosing friends do you look for dependability in their personalities? How and why?

OPTIONAL ENDINGS

Have students complete individual chains with "an action a day for the entire month". Then allow students to take their "dependability chains" home.

Activity 38:   Discussion Cards

Lisa promised to take the trash out every afternoon but today she wants to go to Greg's house. However, she went by her house and took the trash out first. (dependability and responsibility)	If Terry studies his Spelling words on Tuesday he can get ready for the test on Thursday early. Then he will be able to go to Scouts Wednesday afternoon. His mom will be proud! (dependability, trustworthiness, honesty, responsibility, goal setting)	Sheri is supposed to make her bed each morning before coming to school. She really doesn't like to do this but realizes this is a part of her duty as a family member in the house. (dependability, attitude, responsibility, respect toward others, equality)
Rashad is happy to be out of school. It's Saturday and he wants to sleep late. His mom wants him to help rake leaves so he makes a deal to help her after lunch. She agrees. (dependability, cooperation, respect)	Kelly goes in the store to buy bread for her mom. The clerk gave her too much money for her change. She could keep the money, but felt that was not the right thing to do. She returned to tell the clerk. (dependability, honesty, trustworthiness, respect, responsibility)	Trey rides the school bus and has many friends. A new boy has no one to sit with so Trey offers a place beside him. (dependability, kindness, respect, sharing, friendship)
Travis leads a soccer team at recess. Neal is not very good at soccer but wants to play. No one wants Neal on their team. Travis asked Neal to play because he didn't want Neal to feel left out. (dependability, kindness, respect, caring)	Mel has a difficult time getting her tray in the lunchroom because she is in a wheelchair. Cary offers to help each day. (dependability, kindness, caring, cooperation, respect, responsibility)	Have the class write scenarios they have to deal with on the blank cards.

Activity 39:
Dean of Dependability

BRIEF OVERVIEW

As the story about Dean is shared with the class, the important concept of dependability will be discussed and explored. Then students should be albe to apply this character trait to their individual life circumstances.

MATERIALS NEEDED

• Story about Dean (below)

TIME NEEDED

15-20 minutes

OBJECTIVE

Students will recognize the importance of dependable actions and how these actions can affect the re-actions of others toward them.

PROCEDURES

The leader will review the meaning of being DEPENDABLE. Then she/he will read the following story aloud to the class.

Dean was a very good basketball player! Even though he was in the 4th grade he could shoot the ball much better than many of the 6th graders! Dean was quick, he could jump really high, and he had a great eye for the basket.

One day after recess the middle school basketball coach asked Dean if he would like to come to basketball camp during the summer. Dean was so excited! He ran home to ask his parents, but was very disappointed when his dad said, "We'll have to think about it."

"But Dad," Dean begged, "PLEASE, this is the best summer camp I could go to and it doesn't cost very much money. I'll work between now and summer to make some of my own money to help pay for the camp."

Dean's mom then reminded him, "Dean we have depended on you to complete only three chores daily. Do you remember what those are?"

"Of course, Mom."

"Well, I must admit," Dean's mom continued, "I wasn't sure. You were very dependable when we first asked you to make your bed each morning, feed our dog Abby, and take the trash out after supper each night. However, the last two weeks you haven't been as dependable. Instead you've been playing basketball after supper and I've had to feed Abby and take the trash out."

Dean looked at the floor. "Well, I'll do better. Can I have another chance?"

Dean's father then replied, "Yes, we'll give you another chance. The chores are important, but, the **most** important part of this is that we couldn't **depend** on you the last two weeks—nor could Abby! What if Mom hadn't been feeding her?"

"I know, Dad, and I am really sorry. You and Mom will be able to depend on me from now on— I'll make a list of my chores and post it on my bulletin board so I won't forget them."

"Sounds good to me," Mom said. "We'll talk about basketball camp next weekend."

FOLLOW-UP QUESTIONS

1. In the story what were mom and dad most concerned about—the basketball camp, the chores, or Dean's being a more dependable person? Why?

2. What did Dean decide to do to help himself remember his chores?

3. Do you think Dean will get to go to basketball camp? Why or why not?

4. How can you show your teacher that you are a dependable student?

5. How can you show your parents that you are growing to be a more dependable person?

OPTIONAL ENDINGS

K-2 Make a class list of chores, dependable actions, and/or daily routines that students do at home and/or school. Have a class discussion on how these are needed for each student to show good character.

3-5 Ask students to write a paragraph completing this story starter.
    <u>(fill in the blank with a name)</u>   depends on me to...

ATTITUDE TO COMPLETION!

🔑 Keys to a POSITIVE ATTITUDE

🔑 A positive attitude covers many disappointments.

🔑 Plan to have the most positive attitude possible, no matter what the circumstances.

🔑 Good body posture radiates a good attitude to those around you.

🔑 A great attitude is like a taste of your favorite candy - it leaves a delicious taste in your mind and body!

🔑 When a friend is having a bad day, your positive attitude about your friendship will encourage them.

🔑 Walk into your classroom each day with a positive attitude.

🔑 Doing your very best is the most you can expect from yourself.

🔑 Keep an attitude of patience with others and yourself.

🔑 Better attitudes lead to better self-control.

🔑 A forgiving attitude is a peaceful attitude.

Attitude To Completion!

(Sample Parent Letter)

Dear Parent(s)/Guardian(s):

Our class is excited about the lessons in our Character Education series on ATTITUDE! Yes—we are **excited!** With a positive, patient, kind, encouraging attitude our children can feel better about themselves and others.

As a leader in your child's school, I challenge each of us—as adults—to be aware of our attitudes in the presence of our children both at school and home! Please discuss with your child people he/she admires—a family member, friend, athlete, etc. Talk about that person's attitude. Ask questions of your child, like:

- What makes this person special to you?
- Do you think his/her attitude makes you look up to him/her more? Why?
- Do you think his/her attitude has helped make him/her successful as a _____ (ex. housekeeper, teacher, banker, etc.)? Why and how?

Then discuss with your child any areas that an "attitude adjustment" might be helpful in his/her life at home, school, or with friends. You'll be surprised how helpful this thought process will be!

Thanks for your support this year in this most rewarding Character Education program!

My best,

Activity 40:
ATTITUDE CHECK-UP!

BRIEF OVERVIEW

This activity will encourage a positive attitude! It will allow students to recognize that a positive attitude affects goal setting and accomplishment, respect for others, responsibility fulfillment, and much more! Students of all ages will benefit from this activity!

MATERIALS NEEDED

• "Attitude Cheer" sheet

TIME NEEDED

25-30 minutes

OBJECTIVE

Students will recognize positive attitudes in self and others.

PROCEDURES

First the leader will explain a positive attitude (I think I can!) versus a negative attitude (I can't). Lead the class in some "Attitude Cheers". The class will respond with "GO, GO ATTITUDE!" if the cheer is positive and "NO ATTITUDE" if negative.

At this point, the class will discuss the difference between being "up beat" and being down on self and others.

Divide children into small groups to formulate their own cheers to perform in front of the class.

** This activity works well with 3rd-5th graders who then perform for K-2nd graders!

FOLLOW-UP QUESTIONS

1. Who are some people you are around every day that show positive attitudes?
2. How do these people make you feel? Why?
3. Which of your friends shows a positive attitude? Do you?

Activity 40: "Attitude Cheer"

Teacher: Go forward … Go fast …
We will leave our past …
Sit straight … Sit tall …
We won't feel small!

Class: GO, GO ATTITUDE!

Teacher: Get ready … Get set …
New friends we have met …
Trying our best at school …
Really is cool!

Class: GO, GO ATTITUDE!

Teacher: Today is bad …
I really am mad …
I will not try …
I just want to sigh.

Class: NO ATTITUDE!

Teacher: My character is good…
I won't give up…
I take responsibility …
I don't pass the buck!

Class: GO, GO ATTITUDE!

Teacher: My shoulders slump…
My head hangs down…
I don't like school …
I'll be a clown.

Class: NO ATTITUDE!

Activity 41: ATTITUDE WITH LATITUDE

BRIEF OVERVIEW

Using the very familiar literature story, *The Little Engine That Could*, students will recognize the importance of a positive attitude! This lesson will also combine other good character traits such as responsibility (getting the job done), encouragement, goal setting, and courage!

MATERIALS NEEDED

- *The Little Engine That Could* (original story)

TIME NEEDED

30 minutes

OBJECTIVE

The student will recognie the type of attitude it takes to accomplish good things—even when the accomplishment may be very difficult.

PROCEDURES

The leader will introduce the word "ATTITUDE". On the board, students will volunteer different tasks around the class and school that must be done. Then the leader will ask students to talk about how "attitudes" play a part in getting these tasks completed. For example, the floors must be mopped in the lunch room. Or, the bathrooms must be cleaned. Or, classwork must be done in order to learn, etc.

After these have been brainstormed and listed, the leader will ask if some are harder to complete than others. After these have been identified, talk about athletic teams or physical exercises and how these may be difficult sometimes.

Next, the leader will read the familiar story *The Little Engine That Could* to the class.

FOLLOW-UP QUESTIONS

1. How did ATTITUDE help get the job done?
2. Did eveyone have a good attitdue? Why?
3. At the end of the story, how did the attitudes change? Explain!

OPTIONAL ENDINGS

K-2 Have the physical education or drama teacher work with children on a new group activity appropriate to their age levels. Ask these teachers to stress "GOOD ATTITUDES" in their classes in order to complete the activity.

3-5 Start a volunteer program where the older children read to the younger children within the school weekly or every 2 weeks. After the reading is done have a share time in class to talk about how the attitudes of the older students affect the interest of the younger students.

QUOTE TO REMEMBER . . .

Be careful of your thoughts,
for your thoughts become your words;

Be careful of your words,
for your words become your deeds;

Be careful of your deeds,
for your deeds become your habits;

Be careful of your habits,
for your habits become your character;

Be careful of your character,
for your character becomes your destiny.

— Anonymous